Profile 4 – SIOBÁN PIERCY

Profile 4 – SIOBÁN PIERCY

Published as part of Gandon Editions'
PROFILES series on Irish artists (details p47).

ISBN 0946641 900

Editor   John O'Regan

Asst Editor   Nicola Dearey
Design   John O'Regan
                (© Gandon, 1997)
Production   Gandon
Photography   Fergus Bourke
                Audio Visual Services, UCC
Printing   Nicholson & Bass, Belfast

Distributed by Gandon Distribution
and its overseas agents

GANDON EDITIONS
Oysterhaven, Kinsale, Co Cork
tel +353 (0)21-770830 / fax 770755

Cover   *Excerpts from Purgatory*
               screenprint, 1997

Publication grant-aided by
The Arts Council / An Chomhairle Ealaíon
and assisted by
Galway Regional Technical College
Galway Corporation
Galway County Council

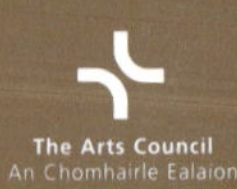

Profile

Siobán Piercy

GANDON EDITIONS

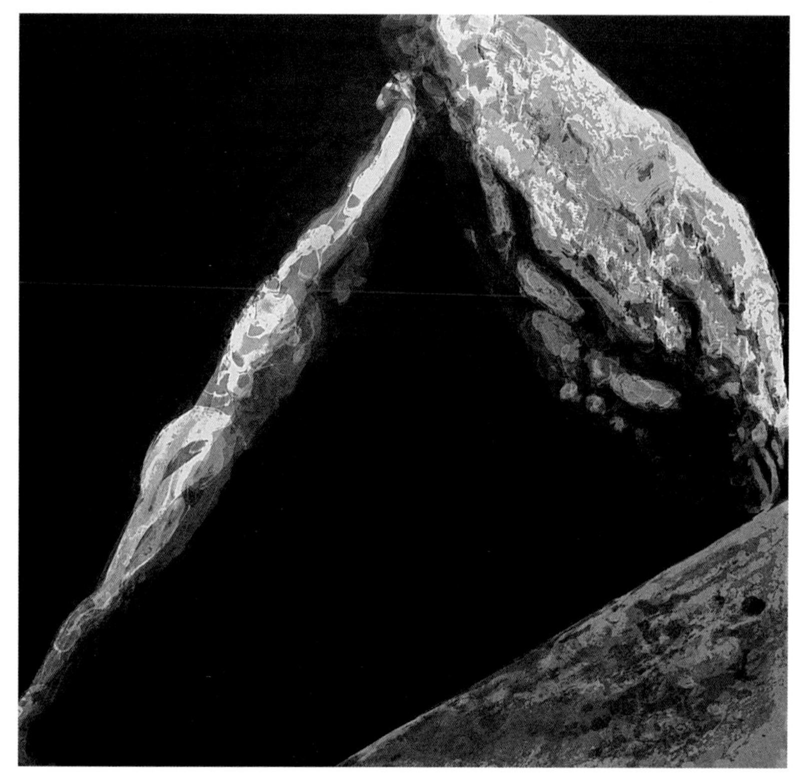

Sisyphus I
1989, screenprint, 18″ x 19″

Angels + Daemons
Siobán Piercy's Cosmography

AIDAN DUNNE

Any approach to Sioban Piercy's work must take account of the titles of her screenprints. What of them? Well, their grammatical formality, their sometimes inordinate length, their catechismal tone, their newspaper-headline phrasing, their air of foreboding, and their underlying rueful, anti-Panglossian conviction that all is not for the best in what is far from the best of all possible worlds ('Can bad weather ever be avoided?'). Furthermore, for all their singular precision, they often sidestep what is, on the face of it, their primary function: to provide us, like the chapter headings of eighteenth-century novels, with a capsule description of what is going on.

Why specify with such pernickety attention to detail when the specifications open up new realms of possibility rather than pinning down the images? But then, something similar happens with the images themselves. Both titles and compositions make it clear that we are dealing with narratives, or at least with clues to narratives, but we cannot take anything beyond that for granted. In at least one case, we are referred to a pre-existing narrative. It is tempting to regard the *Sisyphus* prints as something of a Rosetta stone given the surprisingly direct correspondence that exists between title, image and narrative source. There are several treatments of the subject, all referring to one posthumous episode in Sisyphus's mythology

Consigned to Hades, the legendarily canny king must repeatedly push uphill a boulder that immediately rolls down again – an icon of epic and futile labour that may say a great deal about Piercy's attitude to the often embattled protagonists who inhabit her fictional space.

Elsewhere in that space, though, we don't find such direct and helpful unanimity, and no Sisyphus to guide us like Virgil guiding Dante through the Inferno and the Purgatorio, the sources for Piercy's most recent body of work. This work elucidates the symbiotic relationship between word and image. Its format is the logical culmination of a penchant for elaborate, would-be exegetic titles. Each constituent print is rooted in one of a group of sizeable chunks of text taken from *The Divine Comedy*. The text features prominently in every print, and in some it pervades the entire space, becoming a matrix, a humus from which images spring. It is transcribed in the original Italian, which only a small proportion of any potential audience can be expected to readily understand, a device which has the effect of raising and then thwarting expectations, and is, to that extent, entirely characteristic.

It is certainly characteristic of the practice of holding out the promise of a narrative that is delivered only in a conditional and perhaps contradictory way. There is a graphic demonstration of this in a teasingly titled six-part series of prints, *The Seven Trials* (1994), which refers to episodes in the life of an imagined saint. The pointed lack of narrative closure is ambiguous. On the one hand, we might surmise that we are looking at six surviving works from an original seven; on the other, we know that there are only six pieces in the series, and that the note of inconclusiveness is intended to keep us on our toes.

That quality is central to Piercy's work, pre and post-Italy, but her six-month sojourn in the British School in Rome in 1993 did produce a number of decisive shifts. One reason why we might think that one of the *Trials* succumbed to the ravages of time is because the other six bear the marks of its passing in their surfaces – they look like objects that have weathered the centuries, in terms both of their style and their physical appearance. Italy introduced into Piercy's work a profound sense of the past, of cultural, historical density, and also of temporality, endurance and loss. In fact, when she came to make an exhibition of screenprints and monoprints in which the experiences of Rome were fully assimilated, she called it *Archaeologies*. Individual works have a fragmentary air, like frescoes that have been physically damaged or from which colours have been lost or faded, but it's not only a question of the past. After all, Athenry, where she lives in Co Galway, is itself an ancient town, and its narrow streets abound with clues to an eventful history. It has been suggested that the plain on which Athenry stands, with low horizons and vast, often grey skies, is as responsible for the character of the screenprints made until 1993 as the colour and light of Italy are for work made subsequently.

Italy is also equated with sensuality, and certainly Piercy's work, post-Italy, is distinguished by voluptuous surfaces, with a hugely expanded range of colour and texture and an enhanced interest in pattern. But then, her prints always were sensuous. Pre-Italy, she used a much more restricted palette, but the technique she devised allowed her to develop a wide spectrum of subtle tonal gradations, and the velvety surfaces of her work have tremendous depth and resonance.

Her close-toned, freely brushed technique is particularly appropriate for depicting flesh. In many of her earlier screenprints, the figures are naked and often caught in mid-movement or tensed, expectant. There is a suggestion of physiological research – like Muybridge's photographic studies of human and animal figures in motion – to these images of bodies under pressure. But they are also very sensual presences. The plethora of brushstrokes brilliantly evokes the flexing of skin over a complex armature of muscle and bone, perhaps by conveying something of the quicksilver fluidity of light falling on moving skin, with ripples and flows, mounds and hollows.

When Piercy comes to draw specifically on Dante's great poem of redemption, she is building complex, multi-layered images, but it is striking how close in feeling the content of Canto I of *The Inferno*, and Dante's methodology in the poem, are to her earlier work, in which protagonists are repeatedly pictured in strange, dream-like confrontations with a variety of animals.

The last great, unrealised project of William Blake, an artist and visionary whom Piercy greatly admires, was a commission for one hundred watercolours illustrating *The Divine Comedy*. By the time of his death in 1827, he had produced little more than preparatory work, though a group of engravings that formed part of this are, while unfinished, very powerful. But in terms of finding a visual sympathy with Piercy's printmaking, another of Blake's unfinished projects is interesting. In 1802, and again in 1805, he engraved a number of plates illustrating ballads by William Haley. Each was based on a story involving an animal, and the images depict strange confrontations between people and animals. Remote from the central thread of Blake's concerns, they were made as potboilers, and only a small number of the originally projected series was completed. Nevertheless, they are strikingly visualised, beautifully made engravings, and they have a magical, fairytale atmosphere. Furthermore, they recall his allegorical representations of fragmented consciousness, of individuals at war within themselves, struggling with their 'spectres', their dark or shadow sides – a notion that Piercy develops extensively in her work.

In discussing *The Divine Comedy* in a celebrated essay, TS Eliot makes a number of observations relevant to Piercy's relationship with Dante. Canto I of *The Inferno* sees the poet, midway through his life's journey, lost in a dark forest. As he climbs a mountain, he encounters a leopard, a lion and a she-wolf, and flees. The animals stand for, respectively, lust, pride and avarice, but, notes Eliot, 'It is really better, at the start, not to know or care what they mean.' Instead, he argues, we should consider why Dante chooses to think and write in terms of allegorical images: 'Clear visual images are given much more intensity by having a meaning – we do not need to know what that meaning is, but in our awareness of the image we must be aware that the meaning is there too.'

To say that Piercy's confrontations between humans and animals are dream-like is probably inappropriate by Eliot's reckoning, because part of his argument is that Dante's poem depends on its visionary clarity. It is not a description of a dream, but a direct report of a vision. And it is clear that Piercy's screenprints are not dream-like in the conventional sense of the term either.

In fact, everything about them contrives to present us with a pressing reality. Tellingly, she describes her early paintings as 'super-realist' and 'narrative', in contrast to the formalist climate in which she found herself at college. And there is a compelling naturalism to much of her screenprint work, like the careful simulation of rocky texture in certain of the *Sisyphus* prints.

When she notes an interest in dualism, and particularly in the tensions and oppositions a dualistic view inevitably entail, we can relate that interest readily enough to the divisions that operate in her imagery, rather starkly until around 1993, and less directly since. Up to then, her emblematic motif is the naked human figure under pressure. But it is relatively rare for the figure to exist in a work in isolation. Indeed, the source of the pressure is usually to be found in a division within the composition. More often than not, a print will posit two different kinds of space, with a degree of interaction between them. Each pair of spaces is spare and stylised, but different. One might be open and empty, the other filled with a dense texture that partly obscures whatever resides within it. The difference can be akin to a shift from one element to another, like air to water, or a shift from dense vegetation to open ground. Both shifts might equally relate to a differentiation of kinds of psychic space.

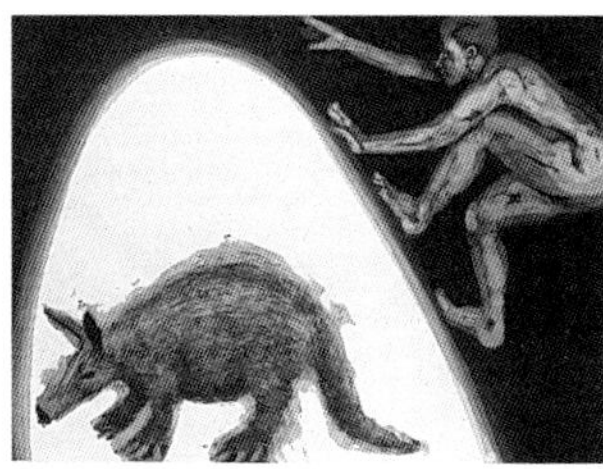

As a basic pattern, we have a human figure on one side and an animal on the other. There are a variety of animals, including, by inference or example, dogs, snakes, wolves, horses, anteaters, fish and hawk-like birds. The essential point is that they are wild animals. Within the work, they interact obliquely with the human figures, but they are in a different realm, and are often represented on a different scale. They enjoy mastery of that realm – they are in their element, unlike the human figures, who frequently seem threatened. It is as if there are two separate but interacting realities at play.

Jung is another name that comes up in relation to Piercy's work, and if we approach her imagery from a Jungian perspective, we can interpret it as relating to individuation, Jung's theory about the processes involved in coming to terms with one's essential, inner self. Perhaps more or less the same correspondence could apply to virtually any theoretical framework describing the attainment of selfhood, but at least one Jungian concept suggests a rationale for her use of male protagonists in her images.

That she does so is to some extent puzzling. Classical psychoanalytical theory is notoriously weak in its applications to female subjects. It prioritises the male experience, as, indeed, Piercy might seem to do in some of her work. It can be argued, however, that, as a woman, her employment of the male body amount to a positive break with artistic convention. More pertinent, perhaps, is Jung's concept of the complementary roles of animus and anima. In essence, for a woman, the animus is the male manifestation, and, perhaps, the male personification of her unconsciousness (just as the anima is the female side of the male). It represents those male aspects of herself that she must accommodate to move towards self-realisation. But, especially given a certain degree of what might be termed a deliberate iconographic vagueness built into Piercy's method, it wouldn't do to be too prescriptive in our reading of her imagery.

Though in conversation she frequently uses the word 'narrative' in relation to her work, it is usually in conjunction with qualifiers like 'imply' or 'hypothetical' or 'mystery' or 'possibility', just as she admits to a religious dimension with terms like 'slightly religious' or 'unspecified', or a preference for a 'familiar as opposed to an unfamiliar religious mythology'. In any case, we can think of the divided compositions as referring to a dualistic split within the world of the individual – between physical and spiritual, consciousness and unconscious, introversion and extroversion, action and passivity, nature and nurture. There is a further twist to the animus-anima idea, which is that each can have a dark pendant, rather like Blake's 'spectre'.

Both title and imagery of *In Pursuit of my Daemon* (1992), with a poised figure against a dark ground on the right, and a striped, horse-like animal cutting through long grass on the left, are reasonably explicit in indicating its concerns. The daemon is, variously, the guiding spirit, the centre of self, the divine spark.

For many cultures, this spirit was embodied in an animal or in some inanimate fetish. In fact, a stone is a common symbol of the self, which casts an interesting light on Piercy's use of the myth of Sisyphus.

Water is a common symbol of inner depths, and fish are ideal exemplars of daemons as dwellers in the deep. When a figure plunges into the water in *The Assent*, it breaches the barrier between the two kinds of space within the composition. It might be diving into the unconscious, assenting to an encounter with its daemon, personified in the form of the fish.

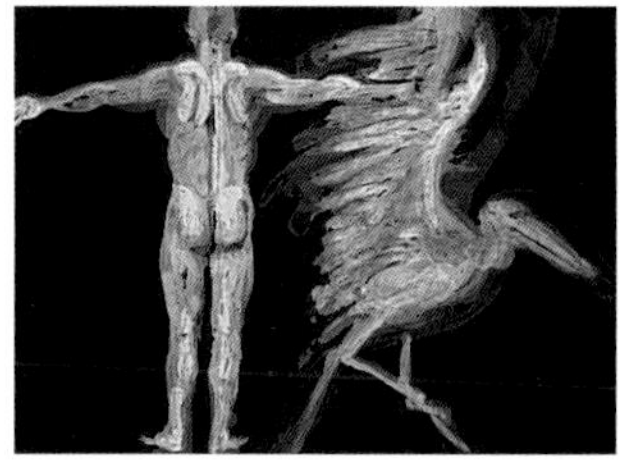

Of course, the point of individuation is that it is a theory attempting to account for a process of becoming. That becoming is directed towards achieving a state of wholeness, towards being a centred individual, and it is reasonable to conclude that Piercy's visualisation of this is the figure of the angel. The angel has several key attributes. He represents a synthesis of human and animal, as the juxtaposition of man and huge bird suggest in *The Angel Anticipates his Wings* (1991). There is a touch of divinity to him, and he mediates between different elements.

Yet, the angel, bowed under the weight of his own formidable wings in *The Angel's Insecurities,* seems afraid of his potential for flight, wary of the possibilities that his status offers, a little like Wim Wenders' angel in *Wings of Desire*, perhaps. He is a fallible, human figure. He is also a tentative first, an initial stab at a hybrid that becomes a staple character in Piercy's repertoire, particularly when she turns her attention to the frescoes of the early Italian Renaissance. Taking our cue from her pre-Italian work, we can deduce that the angels and saints of devotional art become, in Piercy's hands, ordinary individuals struggling to define themselves. This point goes to the heart of that iconographic vagueness of hers, a vagueness that she manufactures, paradoxically enough, through her very precision. Although it is glaringly apparent that a religious vein runs through her work from the earlier screenprints to the most recent, and although it is steeped in Catholic culture, it is hard to say exactly how her work stands in relation to religious belief.

Blake, the visionary, was an impassioned exponent of his own prophetic ideas, but they were often devised and formed on the hoof. Much of his later poetry, with its breathless, formidable complication, reads like theology as reportage. Does Piercy to some extent envy his faith? Or does she follow his example in devising an eclectic religious or mythological system of her own? Only in the sense that what she makes draws on several sources. As *The Seven Trials* indicates, she is more inclined to leave things open. She would, though, be sympathetic to Bronowski's observation that in the prophetic books, Blake's symbols are inconsistent, and that in the end, the books express not a system, but a personality.

Part of the enthusiasm for angels that has become evident in the last few years has to do with a desire for certainty in an increasingly uncertain world. Isaiah Berlin is not the only writer to observe that when rationalism finds itself in the ascendant in the history of civilisations, there is usually a backlash, a rush to irrationalism and mysticism. Yet Piercy's exploration of religious imagery is devoid of revivalist fervour, and there is equally little sign in it of nostalgia for the comfort of dogma.

It is only fair to say that her vagueness isn't vagueness as such. It is more a question of the complexity of her relationship with her subject-matter. It is pretty clear that she is not making devotional art herself; the caustic tone of many of her titles alone underlines that. But, despite the ironic spin that she likes to give to many of those titles, neither is she setting out to debunk the tenets of Catholicism. In a way, she courts misinterpretation. Is she, with postmodernist cynicism, setting us adrift in a sea of interchangeable, indefinitely receding signifiers?

The same question, of course, applies to her use of mythology and other symbolic systems. She continually suggests the possibility of narrative interpretation, but usually steers clear of committing herself to a specific narrative. When the narrative is specific, it is used in a way that introduces additional ambigui-

ties. Yet the indications are that she is far from cynical in her approach. Images and ideas appeal to her precisely because they have exerted, or, indeed, continue to exert a powerful grip on the imagination. It is clearly important to her that we should approach her work without necessarily knowing beforehand, and without trying to pin down unequivocal meanings. As with Dante, it is not the topography of the world that she conjures up that is important, but the emotional force and clarity of the vision and the archetypal familiarity of the imagery.

There is a sting in the tail here. We are not cast adrift into the formal concerns of abstraction. We are not quite free to make what we like of her images. She is not using her sources as a neutral image bank. Rather she is super alert to the fact that every image is inescapably charged with meaning, or meanings, and there is no way of avoiding it.

In some of the more recent work, motifs are individually positioned and liberally seeded in roughly coherent groups – here, a range of leaves from different trees; there, a set of geometrical symbols; some with given, mathematical or cultural meanings; some effectively abstract, but still, in the way they are presented, evocative. The apparent promiscuity of the mix is disconcerting. Without the certainty of a shared, agreed iconography, it is impossible to say that the oak leaf means one thing, and in juxtaposition with maple means another. And to that extent, the effect is a concentrated form of what earlier work implied more obliquely.

The systems of faith and belief to which she refers spring from a need for spiritual expression. They are not malign or false, but they will always disappoint. She cannot allow herself to subscribe to any one system. There are simply too many qualifiers, too many wry disclaimers built into her work to allow any such possibility. What she does evidence is a fascination with the human compulsion to believe, and an interest in what that says about being human. And what is important about the systems of meaning and belief is that they hold a mirror to the individuals and, collectively, to the societies from which they spring. We may look heavenward to find it, but spirituality comes out of human nature.

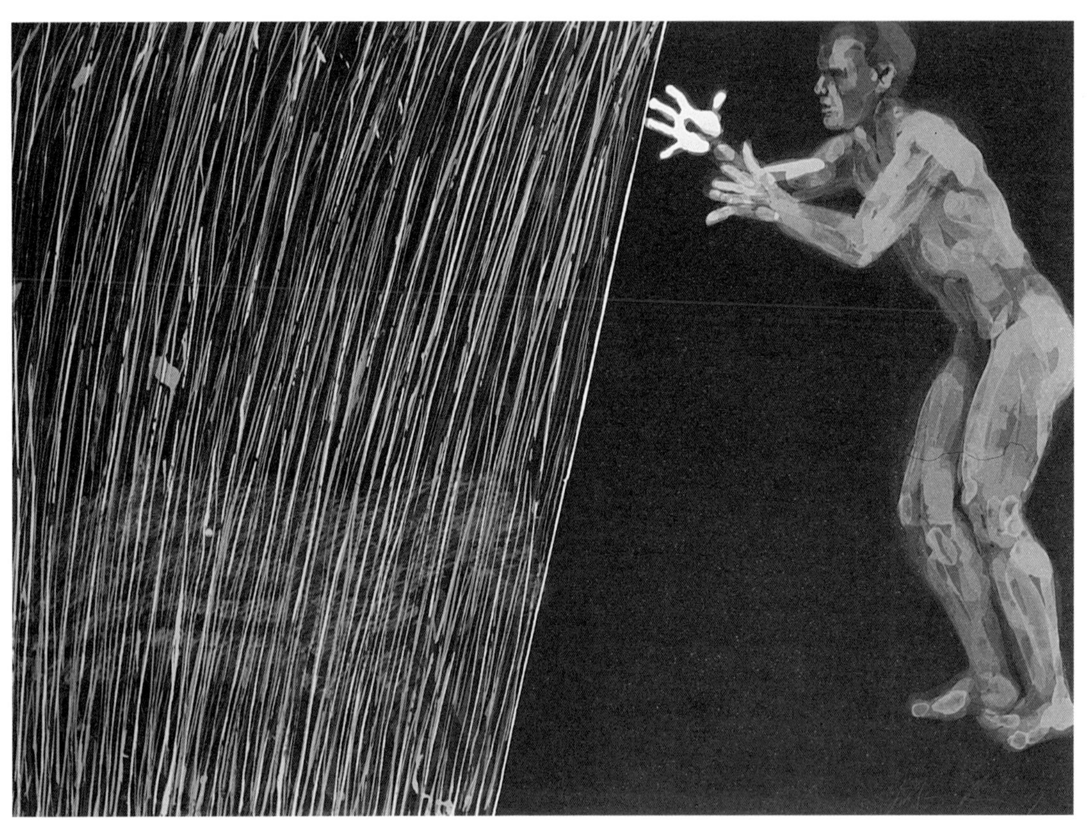

In Pursuit of my Daemon II
screenprint, 1992, 30″ x 45″

A Conversation with the Artist

V E R A   R Y A N

Vera Ryan – You are an art college graduate of the late 1970s. Tell me about the direction of your work over the last twenty years.

Sioban Piercy – What I would like to talk about specifically is the work from 1988 onwards – this was the point when I stopped painting and started to concentrate on printmaking. I had become dissatisfied and frustrated with painting, and felt I could more easily achieve what I wanted through making prints, that I would be able to discover a more personal voice through printmaking.

I made *The Second Passion* in 1989. It was a pivotal piece for me, and points to the work for the next five years and more. I had finally discovered a way of using printmaking that was both painterly and reasonably immediate. It also included the juxtaposition of figure and animal. This theme of opposing forces, of psychological tensions is something that has remained important for me ever since.

How did you find the Crawford College in the seventies?

When I was there, formalism was the order of the day. Notions of content were not really taken very seriously. Ideas of narrative were generally derided at that time. After a short gesture towards abstraction, I found it was not something I could believe in for myself. I felt very strongly that I wanted to make more representational images and deal directly with the content. I made that commitment and haven't changed from that position.

How has teaching art full-time for nearly twenty years in Galway Regional Technical College affected your work?

Art teaching is very stimulating and demanding. It stretches you. Students will force you to evaluate your own attitudes. I find that very healthy. I think it has forced me to consider many diverse approaches to art.

Do you think teaching draws on the same energy source as making art?

It does drain your creative energy. You can talk away a lot of your own ideas, and it can be difficult to maintain a focus on your work because the time available can be very disjointed.

And how does it feel as an artist to work in the Galway region?

Perhaps working in Galway, one does feel a little removed from what is described as 'mainstream' or international art. I think that this has led me to search for an art that is more personal, individual, and perhaps more independent of superficial trends. One of the things I like about making prints is that it's a way of reaching an audience very directly; they don't have to be part of the mainstream to be seen. They can be almost subversive. Goya did that with his prints.

Are printmakers marginalised?

Printmaking in Ireland is certainly developing very well. However, I feel there remains an underlying prejudice against print. It's not considered on the same terms as painting and sculpture.

Are people encouraged to look at the work as technique or as artefact?

Printmakers are as much at fault as anyone in over-emphasising technique. How a print is made is discussed more often than particular issues or ideas, whereas painters or sculptors would never talk exclusively about process or technique, if at all. This emphasis on craft can be a way to avoid tackling the more difficult questions of art-making, and is, in my view, printmaking's great weakness. Many critics and viewers, and even artists, cannot see past the craft; they cannot see printmaking as a means to an end. But I believe this attitude is changing rapidly, and I feel strongly that it should.

I think of you mainly as a screenprinter?

At the Crawford I majored in painting, and I took printmaking – screenprinting in particular – as a second subject. I also worked part-time as a commercial screenprinter while a student, printing T-shirts and that sort of thing, to put myself through college. I gained a great deal of technical experience from this, and became quite proficient in the medium. When I was looking for an alternative to painting, I quite naturally thought of screenprinting, but I have deliberately avoided the hard edge, flat colour that usually typifies screenprinting, and sought out ways of using the medium that are, perhaps, closer to painting and drawing. In the last year, I have changed from using oil-based to water-based inks. This has forced me to change the way I have been working, and it has taken me a long time to come to grips with these new inks, but the oil-based inks and, in particular, the thinners used with them are so unhealthy that I didn't want to continue using them.

You have also made etchings.

I made two etchings based on the Angelus: *The Appearance of the Angel* is one, the other is *The Message*, and is more explicitly about male/female relationships. When I was in London, I had the opportunity to learn other forms of printmaking – lithography as well as etching, but I keep coming back to screenprinting. I still find it the most versatile method of making prints.

Did you work from the stuffed bird in the studio for the wings in The Angel's Insecurities?

Yes, I used it specifically as reference for this print and for *The Small Joy*. For other prints that depict animals and birds, I used various sources: naturalist books are good, and I particularly like natural history museums. *The Small Joy* was made before *The Angel's Insecurities*. It has two figures – a man holding a bird and a female watching. Then I decided to put man and bird together to make a winged figure. The arrival of the angel motif was a kind of natural progression rather than a conscious choice of it as an image.

The animal in the prints is a point of contrast, a way of emphasising our humanity, our difference from animals, but it can also function in the opposite way. It can make us more aware of our animalistic natures; it can symbolise nature in ourselves. It can become a metaphor for a state of mind or an emotion.

When I started making these prints, I also began to increase the scale to give the images greater physical presence. The largest I have made are five foot by three and a half.

Do you work in small editions? Do you get help from print technicians?

No, I don't get help from print technicians; my studio is at home. And yes, I work in small editions, usually not more than ten. Because of the techniques I use, it's difficult or impossible to make long runs. The stencils just won't last. I like to work in an immediate and direct way, and if I were to do long editions, I would have to use photographic techniques, which are far more laborious and less spontaneous.

Would it be correct to suggest that the work has taken on a new energy since the year you spent recently in the Royal College of Art in London?

The period in the RCA was a period to consolidate what I had been working on up to that point. The dark, flat background connects the pre-London and the London work visually. The work from 1988 to 1993 had two juxtaposed images, usually a figure and a rock, or a figure and a figure, or a figure and an animal. The shift from painting to screenprinting focused my work; that came around 1988 or '89, before London. I've had a clear direction for the ten years or so since then.

Your work isn't autobiographical, is it? Yet your use of these figure-based narratives seems to be too urgent and energetic to be impersonal.

The impetus for the work is personal. It is based on personal experience of the world. But it is not necessarily factual; it is also a fabrication, in the same way a writer's story doesn't have to be autobiographical even though the story is based on what he or she knows.

Images of conflict recur, do they?

Yes. In the late 1980s to early '90s, images of opposing forces were the main theme. It is not so clear-cut now, it's not a matter of a simple duality. Earlier, I was specifically interested in theories of duality and how everything defines itself through its opposite. I wrote my RCA thesis on the idea of dualism, and I researched it as a theme in philosophy and religion. It is vast, it's overwhelming! It's something fundamental to our perceptions of ourselves and our sense of identity.

Yet there is little direct confrontation?

All the images then depicted things on the point of happening, the moment before resolution. The images remained as potentials. They could resolve themselves in several ways.

Through my research, I discovered I have a great affinity with William Blake, particularly as a printmaker. His relationship to printmaking was a fundamental part of his work. It related to his notion of the spiritual and the physical. For him, printmaking was the product of an interaction between his spiritual and imaginative elements and the physical world.

Printmaking is so physical. When you make a print, it is you interacting with your medium. Blake trained as an engraver, but it was the duality between the imagination or the spirit and printmaking – which is of the physical world – that was his art.

What other printmakers do you admire?

One person I am very influenced by at the moment is Paladino, who isn't primarily a printmaker. But the artists I've been looking at mostly are painters from the early Renaissance. Giotto is such a strong influence. The way Giotto used blue as a visual theme to connect the panels is so striking when you're in the Scrovegni Chapel in Padua. It changed my attitude to colour. His colour palette was quite restricted, and this gave a wonderful consistency to the work.

What other art forms stimulate you?

Literature. Through my husband's work, I have an opportunity to discuss many literary ideas. I tend to read books which deal with ideas rather than straightforward novels, which may seem strange given the narrative tendencies in my work. I have also begun to incorporate certain literary texts into my work.

Are you interested in psychoanalysis?

Yes. I've read Freud but I'm probably more interested in Jung. Certainly I'm interested in ideas of archetypes and Jung's theories on the symbolism of various religions. He wrote a series of books on the underlying significance of alchemy, some of which I've read over the years.

Is a specifically female experience central to the work? It is seldom without male or female figures, the females seldom being alone.

My work is not consciously about the female experience. It explores different psychological states. I probably feel these experiences are universal. Some of the images I make do touch on a particular female experience, but the female is not a dominant concern. The way I would perceive myself is as an artist who is a woman. Perhaps it is that I think there are a lot of women dealing with the exclusively female perspective. I do not root my identity exclusively in my sexuality.

Or nationality?

No, but when I am in Ireland, I'm often considered English, and in England, I'm considered Irish. Questions of nationality are not an overt consideration in the work either. Perhaps if you wanted to analyse it, you could trace my obsession with conflicting forces to my mixed background. But I have not focused on this in any political way.

Perhaps you deal with personal issues through myth?

The work is based on personal experience. Some of the mythologies are personally important, but I don't believe they are exclusively mine. It comes down to the archetypal image. Every individual can generate a range of images which are personal to them, but many of these images will be common to humanity.

You worked intensely with the figure ten years ago or so? Apart from the model, is the art historical figure, so to speak, important as a source?

Prior to 1993, the muscular figures in my work could be associated with the later Renaissance, for example, with Michelangelo. That wasn't a conscious influence. Then in 1993, the early Renaissance became the paramount influence, consciously.

I like the way Giotto arranged the figure on the picture plane. In my earlier work, there was a single viewpoint, but when I saw Giotto's work, I realised that I preferred the way in which he allowed the narrative to be paramount. It was always more important to organise the picture plane in a way that made the narrative work, rather than create the illusion of space. In the earlier prints, I was interested in subtle shifts of tone and temperature, like a warm grey against a cool grey. Somebody once commented that they could see where my colour came from. The grey subtleties came from the colours of the Galway landscape. But in Italy I was knocked out by the colours of Giotto. Those colours have stayed with me since.

In Italy I did a great deal of drawing, not so much printmaking. I wanted to see and to absorb, not be in the studio. There was so much to assimilate; it took a year or so for me to absorb what I had seen. In 1994 it started to come out in the work, and then there was a dramatic change.

Do you usually rely on sketchbooks, apart from in Italy?

I do work in sketchbooks, but many of the ideas resolve themselves through the printing process and come from the work itself.

Is it true to say that life drawing is important in the recent work? Do you still work from the model, or from photos?

In the past I have worked referring very specifically to drawings or photos, but less so now. I work more from memory and imagination. I find that liberating. I am not as dependent now on something I have received as a visual fact.

Did you do life drawing when you were a student in the Crawford?

I did, regularly. For my work, I found it essential to build up a knowledge of the human figure through observational drawing. I do life drawing when I can. I had access to a model in the RCA, and also to a motor-drive camera with which I could record a sequence of photos of someone moving, so I built up my own reference. Before the RCA, I used the Muybridge series of photographs as reference material for figures in motion.

You've worked outside Ireland quite a lot in the 1990s.

I spent time in London from 1990 to '92 for my MA, and in 1993, I won a scholarship in printmaking at the British School in Rome for six months. When you go to Italy it is all so familiar; it's like coming home to something. I suppose it's the same for many artists.

Do you mean from looking at things in books?

Yes. But it's more complex than that; it connects to Christian mythology. In Ireland, images of Christianity are so pervasive that when you go to Italy it's like rediscovering these images.

Did you grow up in Ireland?

No, not entirely. My family came to Ireland in the sixties. My father was English and my mother is Irish, from Kilkenny. She comes from a Catholic Irish background, he from a Church of England, English background.

Did you turn to religious imagery soon after returning from Italy?

Before going to Italy, I was interested in mythology, but I had overlooked Christian mythology, which now seem more relevant to me than, say, Greek or Indian mythology. I had already used saints and martyrs in *Purgatory of the Virtuous* (1989) and other works, but 1994 was when I shifted more directly towards religious imagery.

Some of my images have quotes from the early Renaissance frescoes; the artists themselves have quoted from one another. In my work, the figure might be taken from one fresco, and other elements added. I particularly liked the fragments of frescoes, more than the complete narratives. I like the weathered frescoes; I loved the images when they were nearly worn away and you had to piece them together in your imagination. Traces of colour rather than intense colour feature in the work made after the Italian trip.

I also started to introduce other visual elements, like the line drawing in *Fear of Being Alone* and *The wolf pretends...* I was dealing with space in a different way, in multiple perspectival spaces. But the immediate ones are still quite dark, as in *Fear of Being Alone*. There was a dramatic change after about a year. Rather than using subtleties in dark colours, I shifted the tone up the scale. They were all much lighter; there were subtleties of pale colours and light colours rather than dark subtleties.

Pattern too became an element.

Yes. The early ones and the London ones were bleak, I suppose.

Do you cut off your images at this stage, to suggest a fragment?

Yes, to a certain extent, but not exclusively. If you look at, say, *Secret Revelations* it has the animal and the figure, as in the earlier work, and is not like a fragment; it's self-contained. In *Story of the Mantle*, which has the dog and the figure as well as the cloak, I am alluding to the way in which the Renaissance artists would tell a story through a series of panels, but the story is my own. There are two panels; one image works off the other to suggest possible narratives. I like the idea of the saint as protagonist. In *The Seven Trials*, a series of works in the UCC Collection, there are six panels – two in each print. Each panel represents an episode or trial in a potential saint's life.

Is there a consistency to your work?

The underlying concerns are consistent, although the approach has shifted, obviously. The connecting factor is the concern with narrative and the idea of trying to put together images that have a powerful charge and that provoke a response in many different ways, whether psychological or intellectual or emotional. Creating narratives that engage the viewer rather than being merely descriptive is the important thing. They are deliberately ambiguous. I want to create potent images that can function on many levels – emotional, intellectual, visual.

In the London period, what was being expressed was a greater psychological tension – one of opposing forces. These tensions and internal struggles are still there in the Italian work, but they have become more subtle and complex in their expression.

The work around the London period seems less serene than the work around the Italian period.

Being in London was stressful, for many reasons, but particularly financial. The scholarship in Italy was a real luxury. I didn't have to worry about anything; even meals were provided.

The current work integrates text into the image. Are the prints less narrative when you use text?

The titles have always been an essential part of the work, not just a means of identifying a piece. But I wanted to find a way to incorporate language more directly into my work. I have begun to use text, but not in a way that gives a direct narrative. The images interact with the text to precipitate a range of meanings. The text in these recent prints is not my own; they are quotes from Dante's *Divine Comedy*.

Which fascinated Blake.

Yes. His interpretation of Christianity was a very personal one to him, and one I have more empathy with than the orthodox one.

The images I use for *The Inferno* and *Purgatorio* are more particular to me, and are overlaid on the text or are behind it. They are not illustrations of the narrative, but images that have powerful connotations and resonance which are added to by the presence of a text and a title. The red feather for example, which can evoke ideas of flight or flames in opposition to the cube and the text, has the potential to generate many meanings.

Along the line of weight and weightlessness, dualities?

The geometric forms are fabrications of the human mind which represent ways of ordering human thought and perception, or of ordering nature. The text from Dante is at the gateway to Hell, which translates as 'Abandon every Hope ye that Enter'. It is overlaid on geometric forms, and sets up another dynamic. I am using my own titles, as well as the quotes from Dante. This creates an important dimension in the reading of the work. The quotations are in Italian, so people can engage with them at a purely visual level or else tease out the translations, if they can.

How do you see your work progressing from here?

My work is a continual search for more effective ways to represent my fundamental concerns, a search for images that are both personal and archetypal, for pictorial narratives that communicate something of human experience. These preoccupations have always been important to my work, and while they are continually refined and modified, they are still intrinsically the same as when I began my career. I can't imagine that I will stop this search.

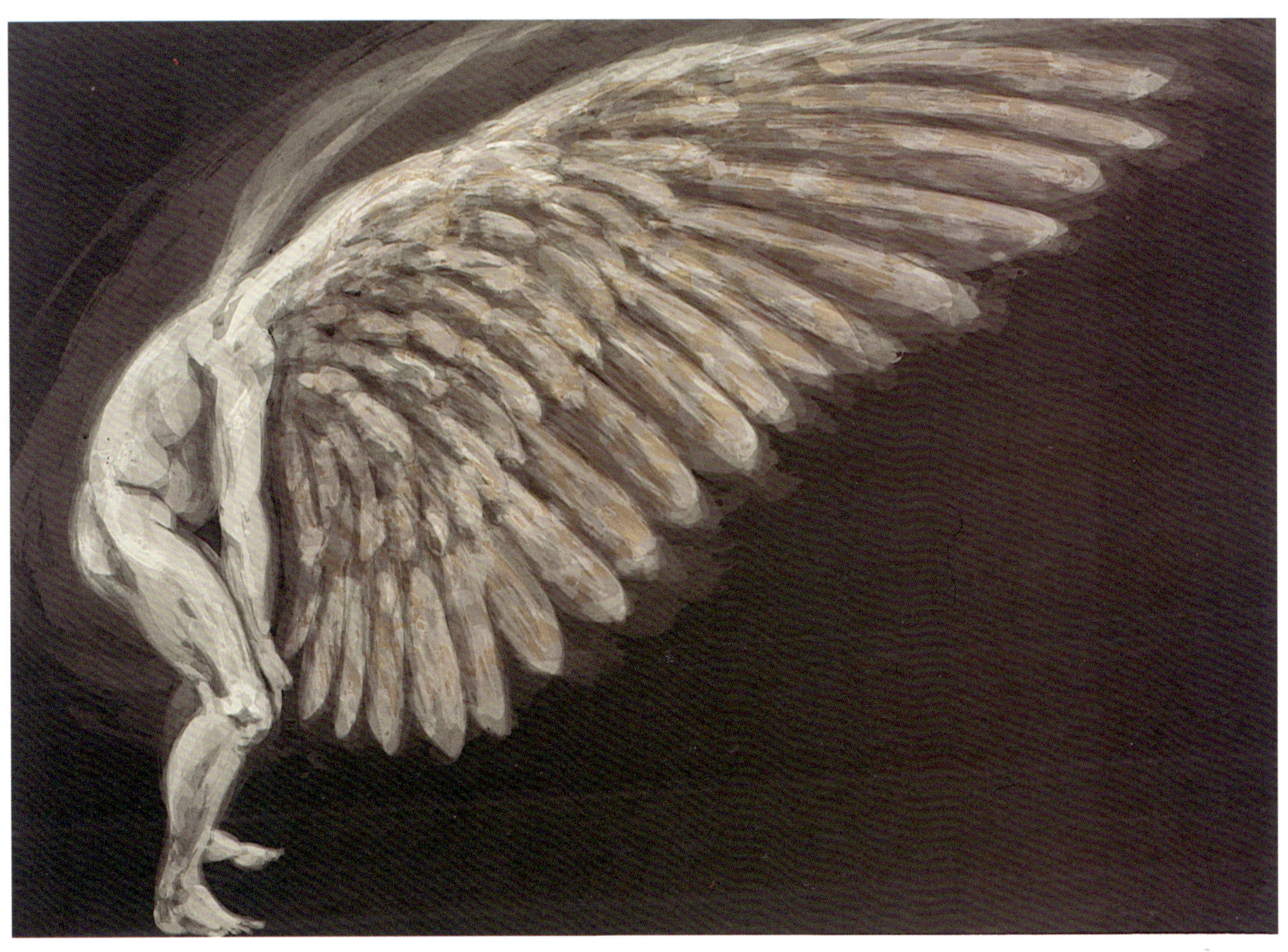

The Angel's Insecurities
1991, screenprint, 30" x 45"

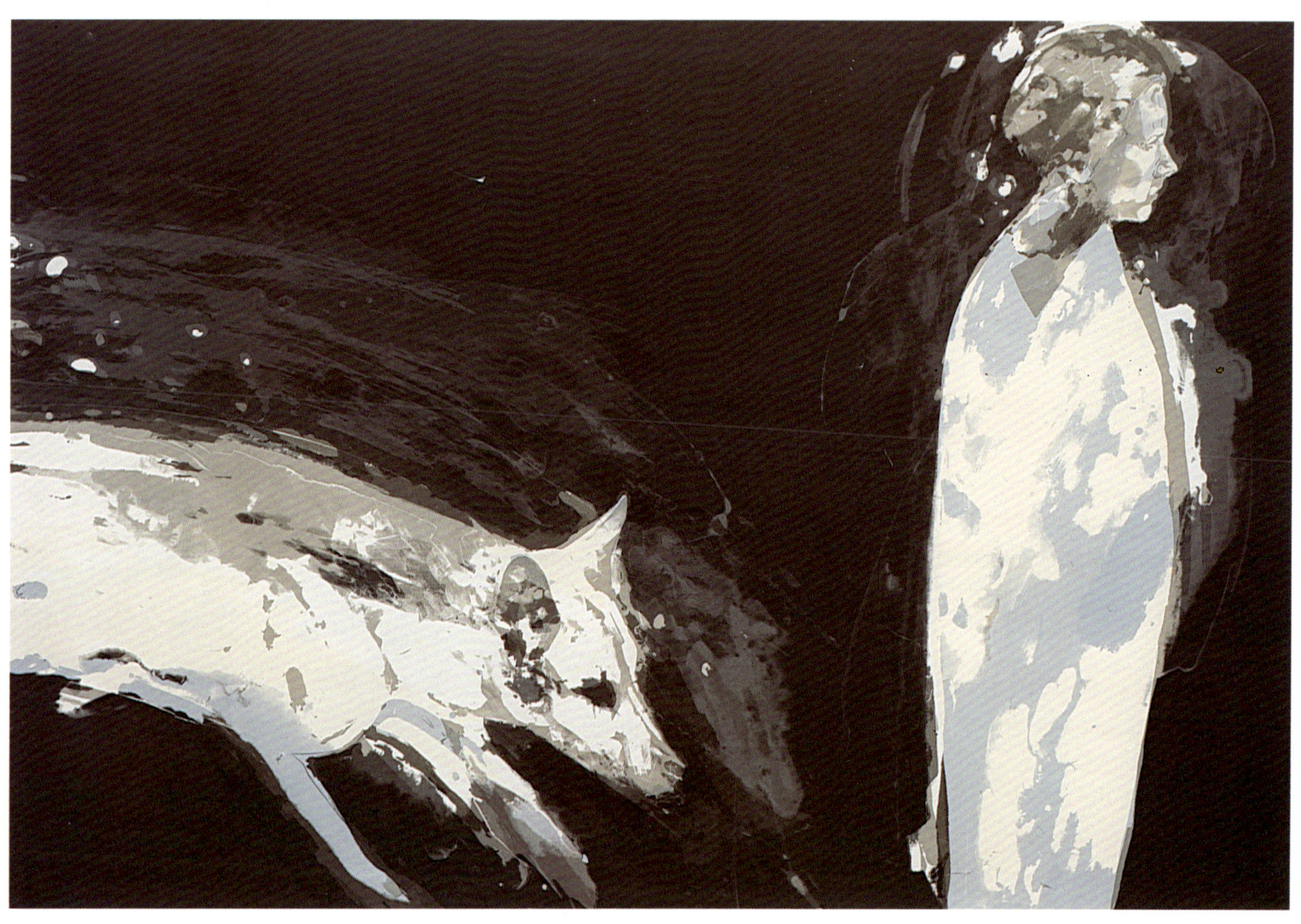

The Second Passion
1989, screenprint, 22″ x 30″

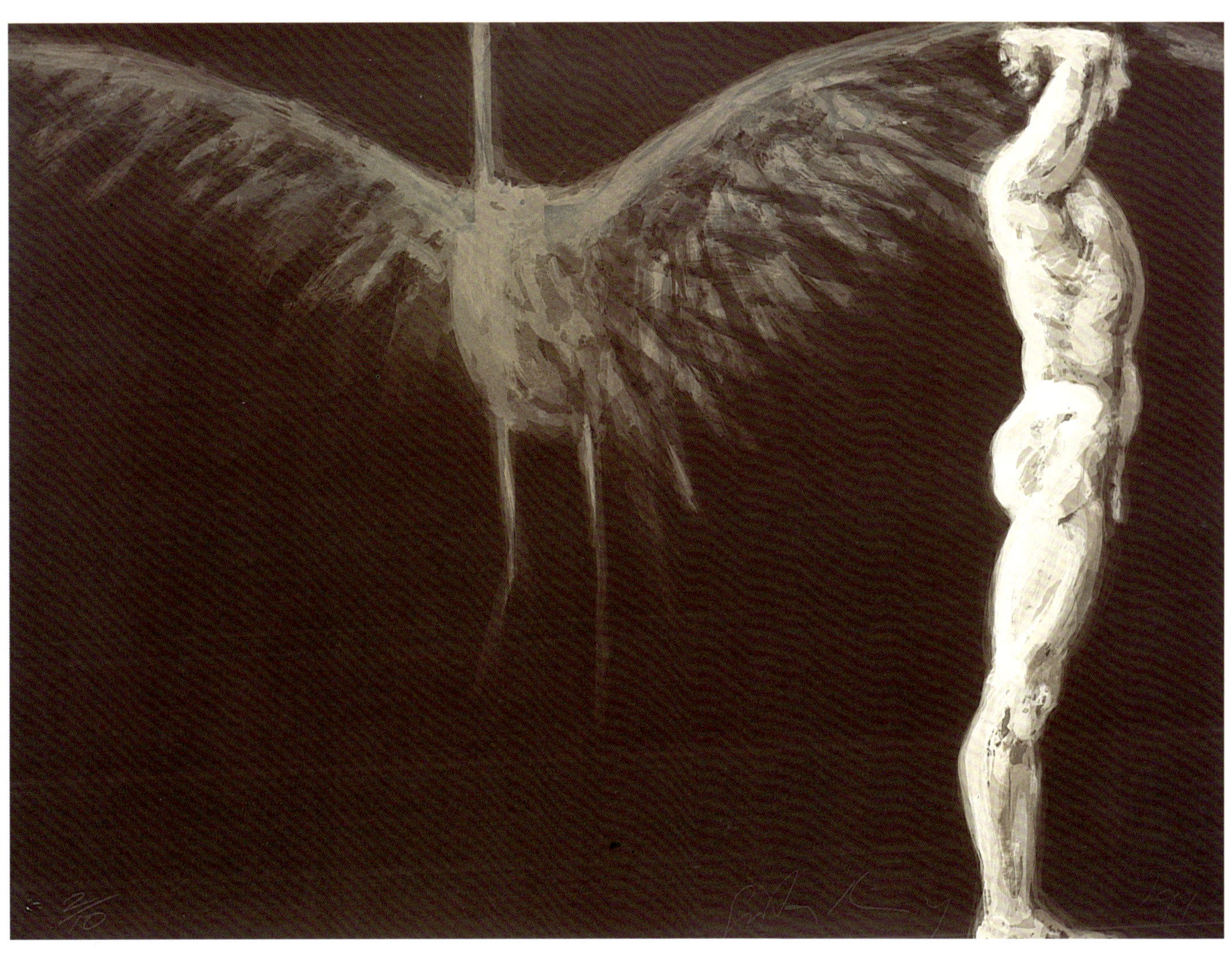

An Angel Anticipates his Wings I
1991, screenprint, 22" x 30"

A Saint Awaiting (a second) Temptation
1992, screenprint, 60" x 40"

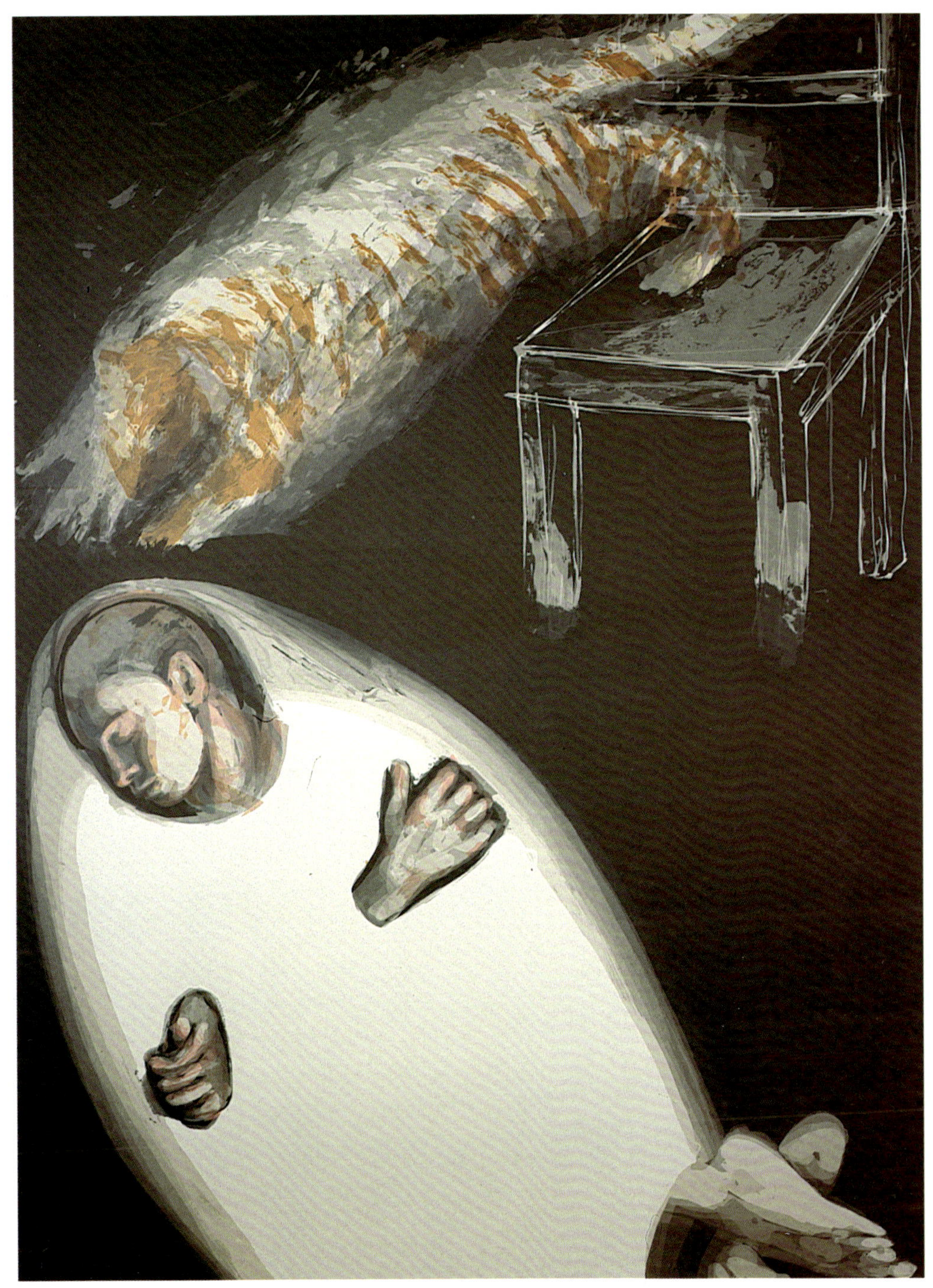

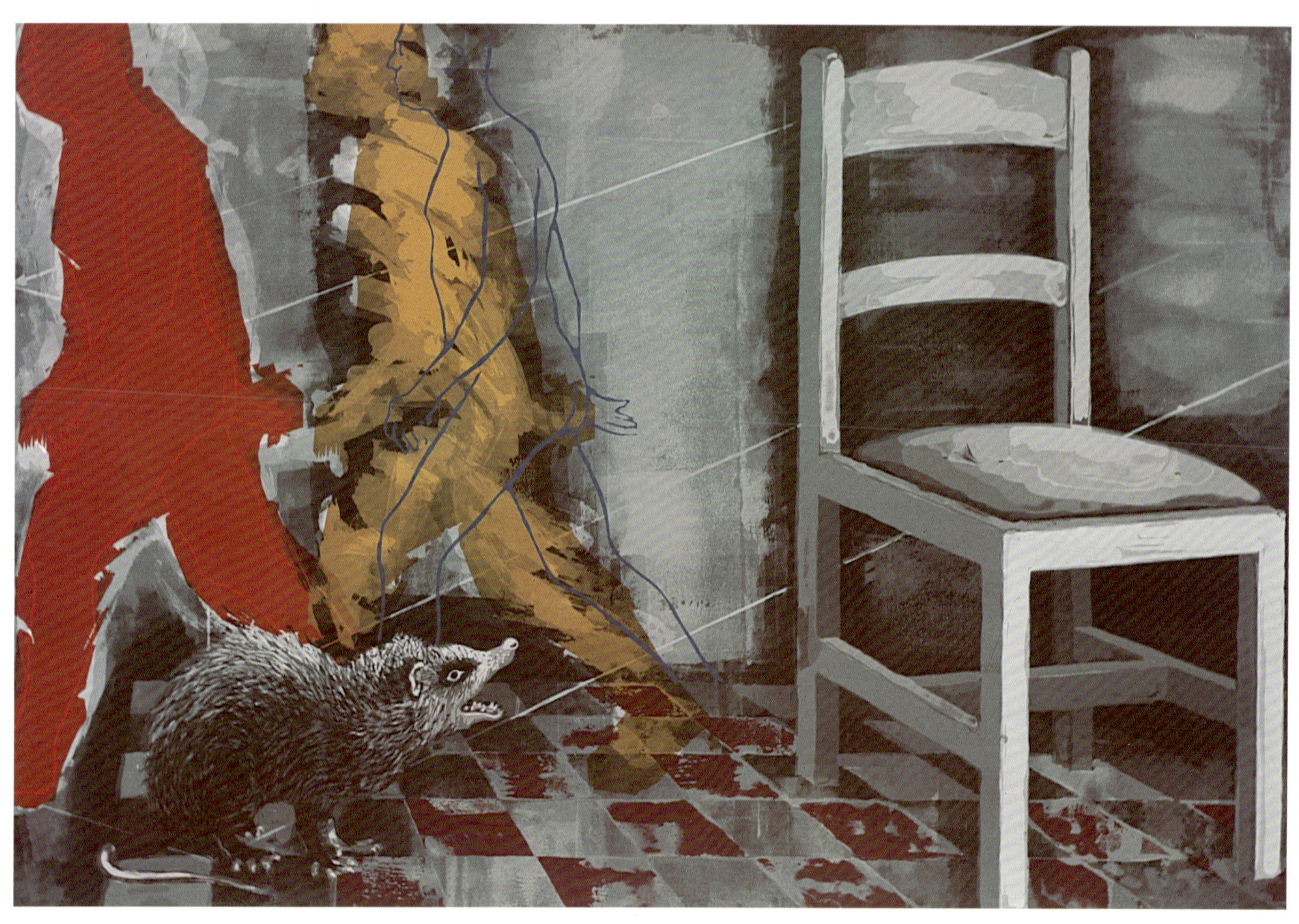

Fear of Being Alone
1993, screenprint, 30" x 45"

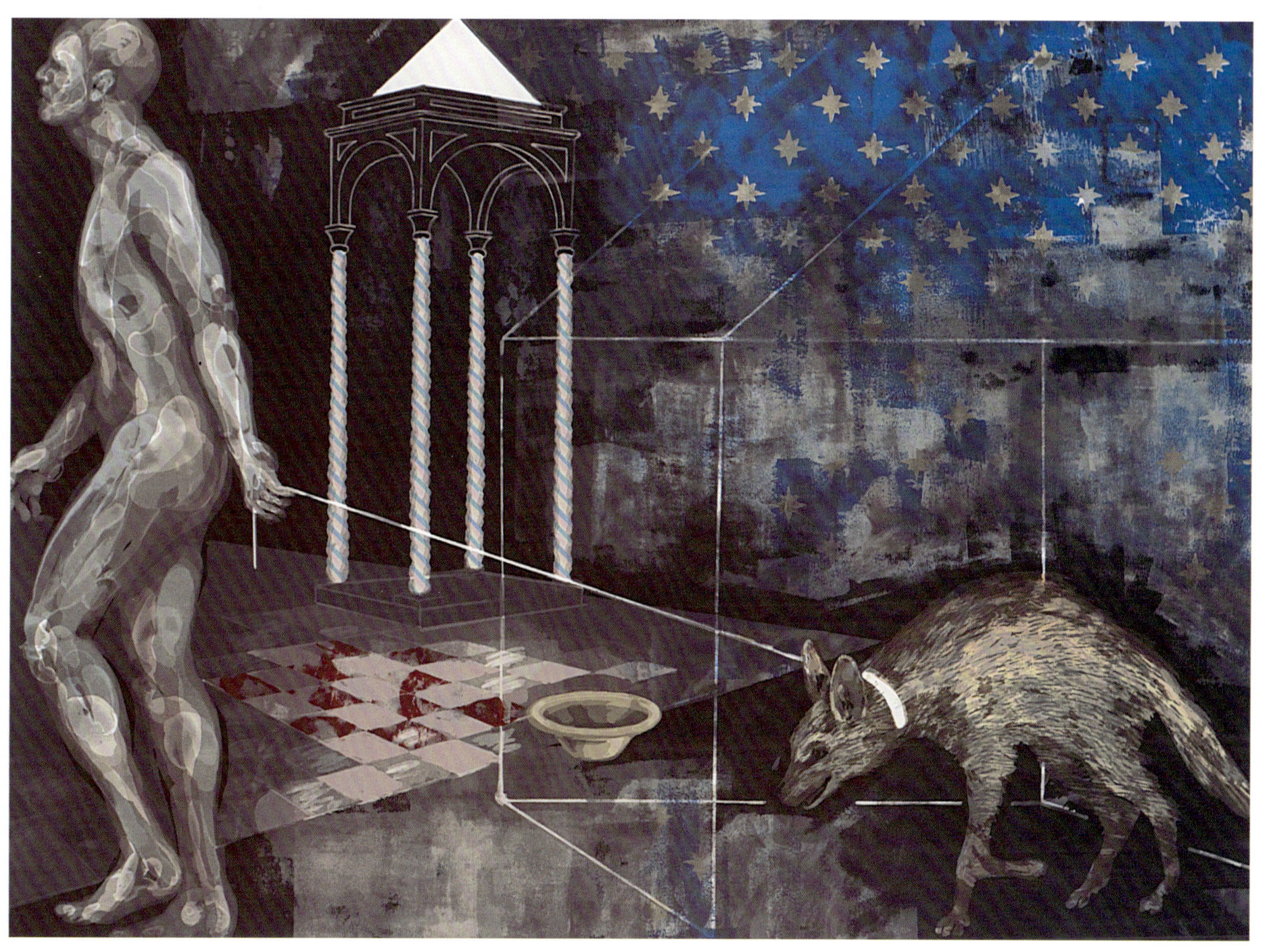

The wolf pretends she is a tame dog
in order to sneak into the fold
1993, screenprint, 30" x 40"

An Archaeology
1994, screenprint, 30" x 45"

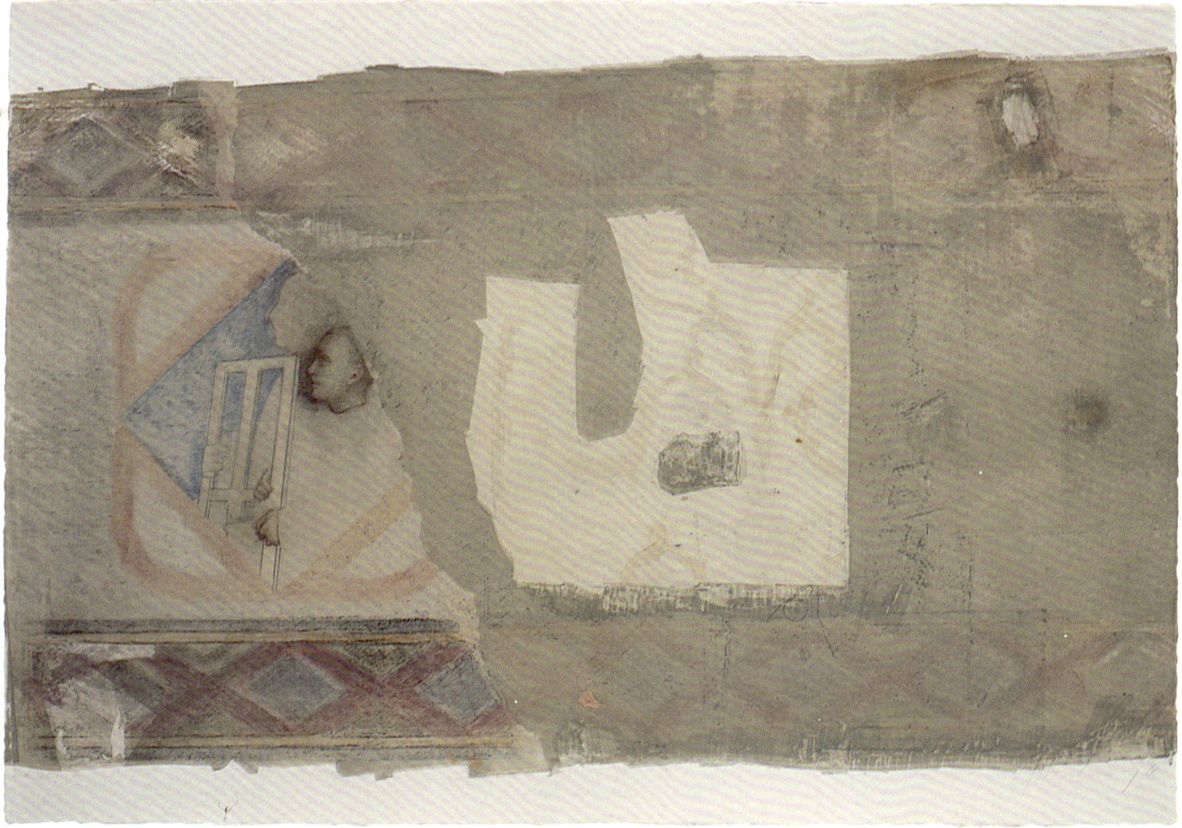

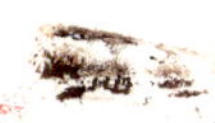

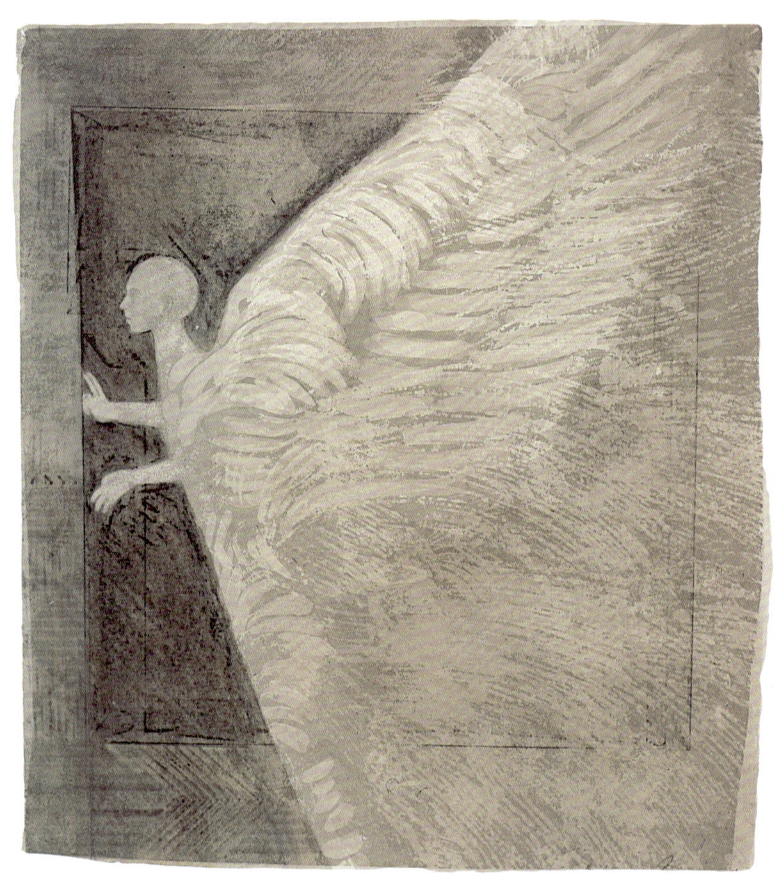

Announcing Angel
1994, screenprint, 18″ x 18″

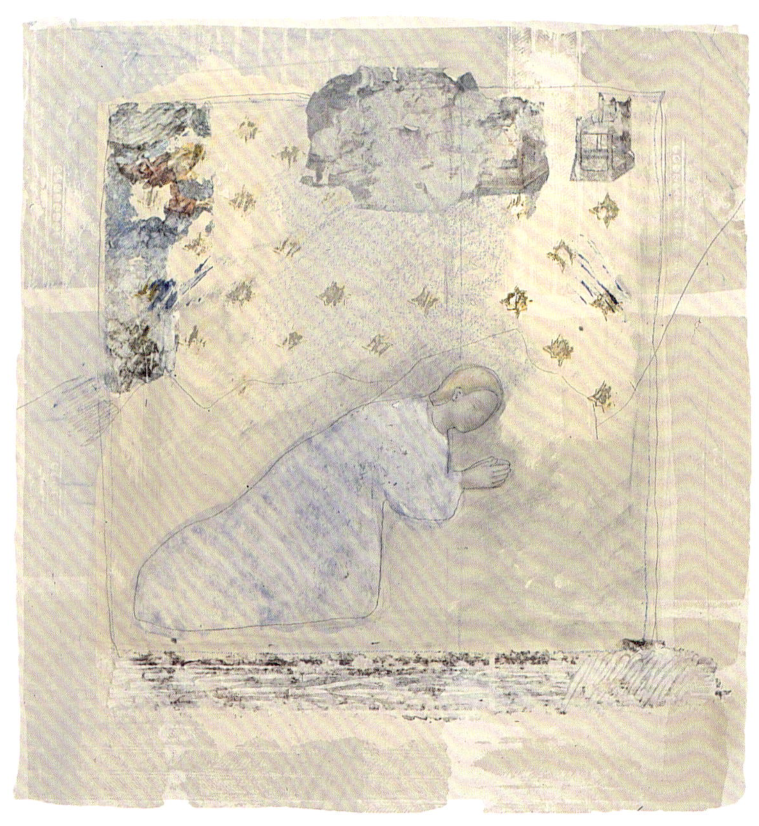

The Reward is the Temptation'
1994, screenprint, 18" x 18"

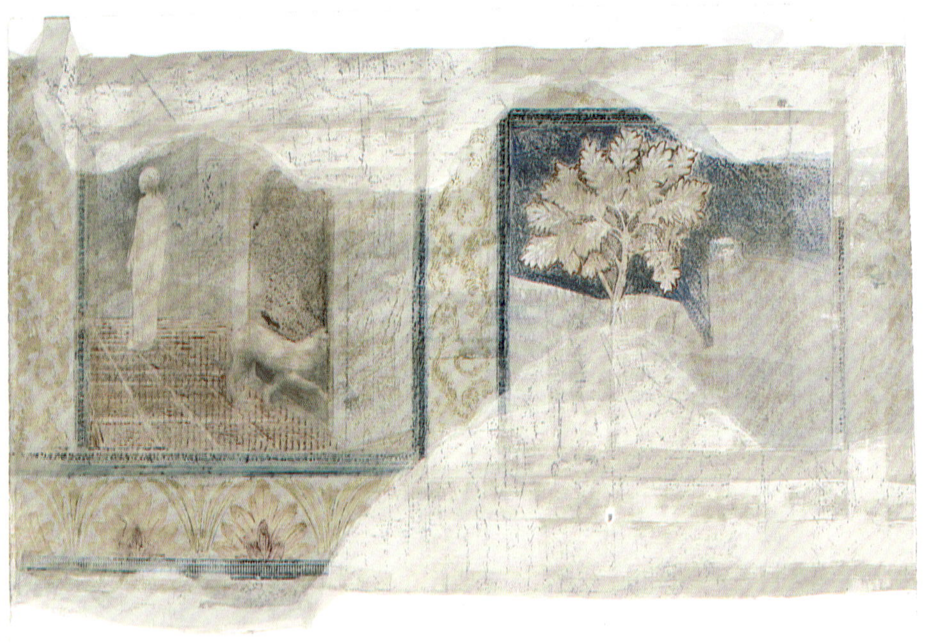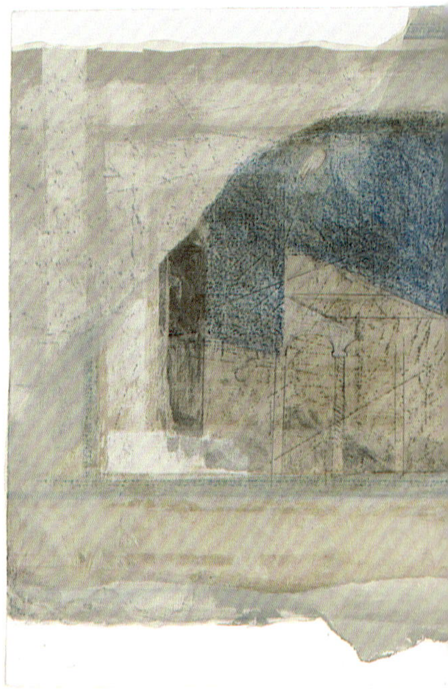

The Seven Trials
1994, set of three screenprints, each 30" x 45"

I *Courage to Face Temptation*
II *Fear of Knowledge*

III *Fear of Absence*
IV *The Temptation of Heavenly Reward*

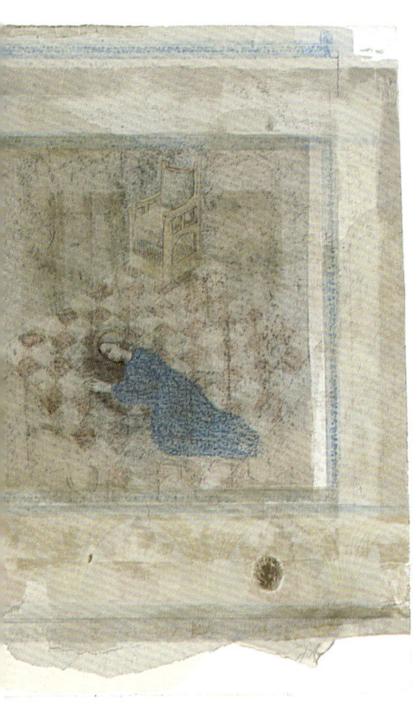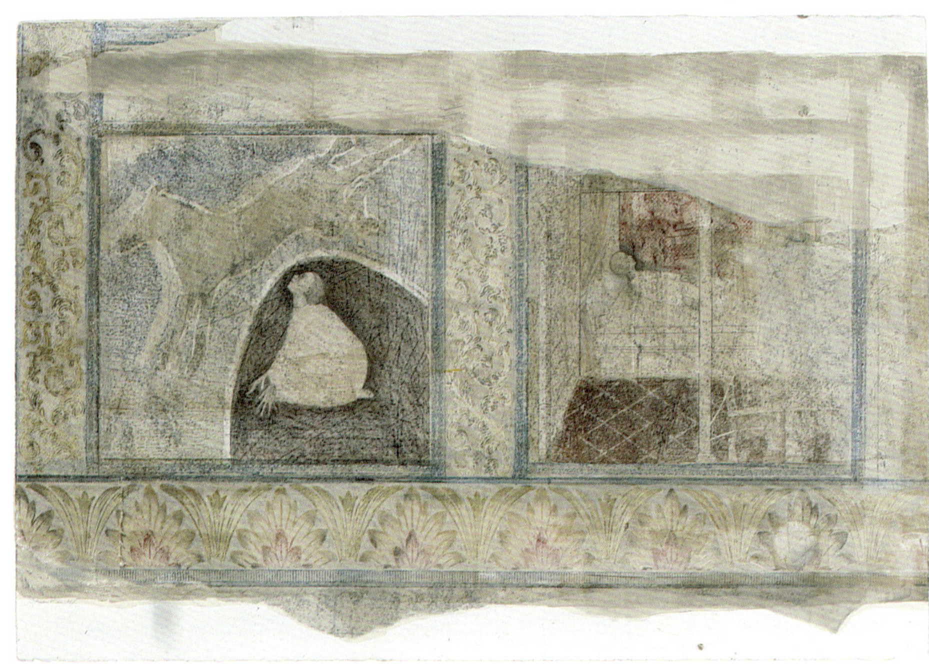

V *Doubt of Visions (of the Future)*
VI *The Temptation to Embrace Death*

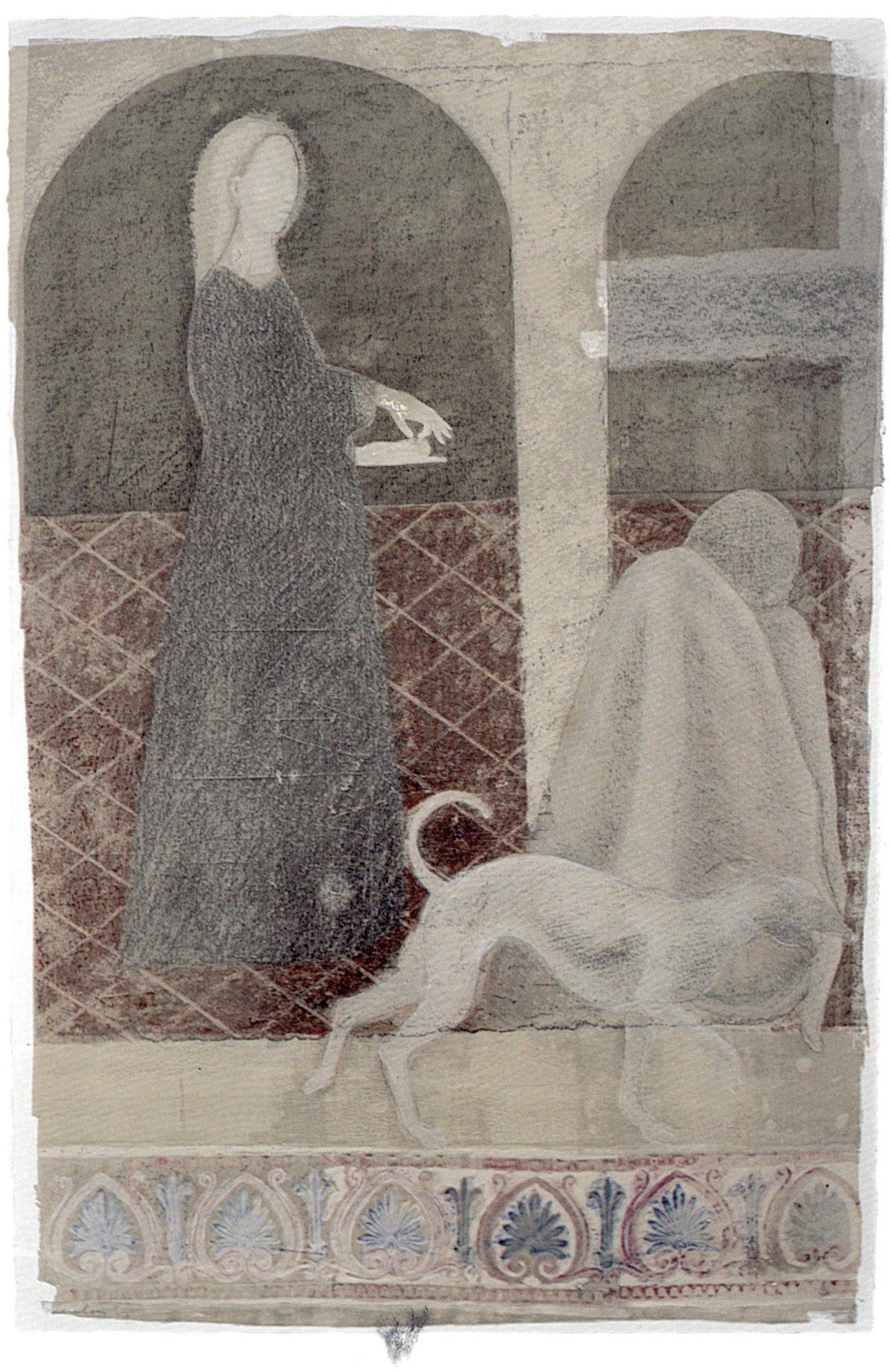

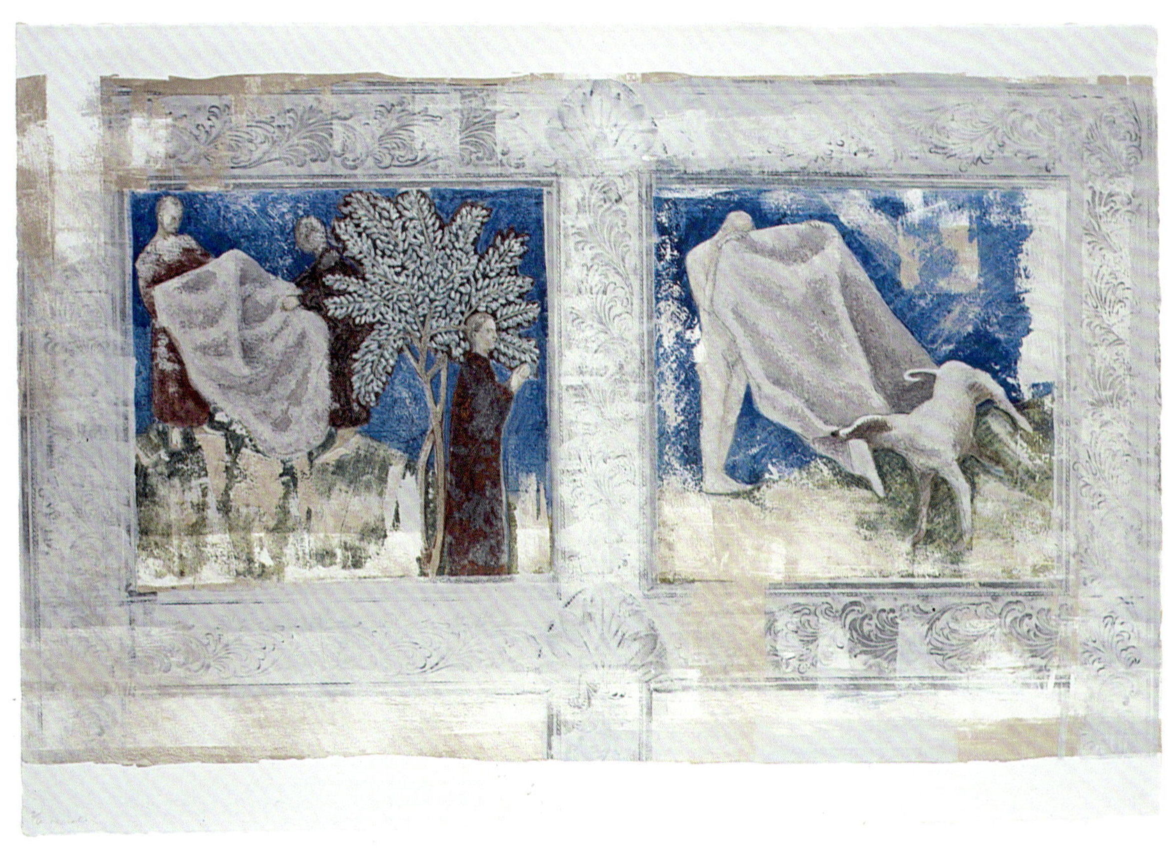

The Story of the Mantle
1996, screenprint, 30″ x 45″

opposite
Secret Revelations Held Dear
1995, screenprint, 45″ x 30″

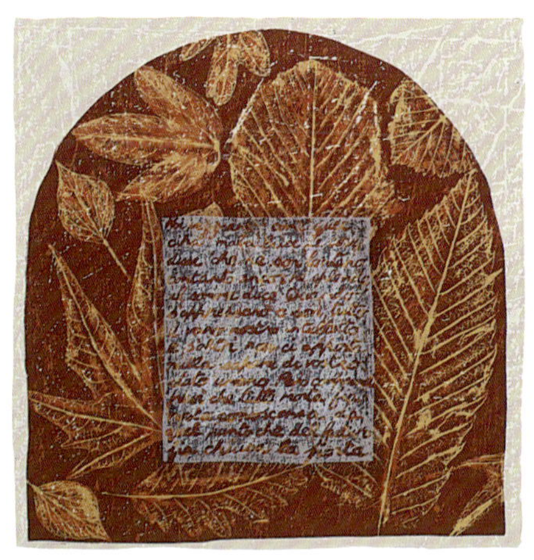 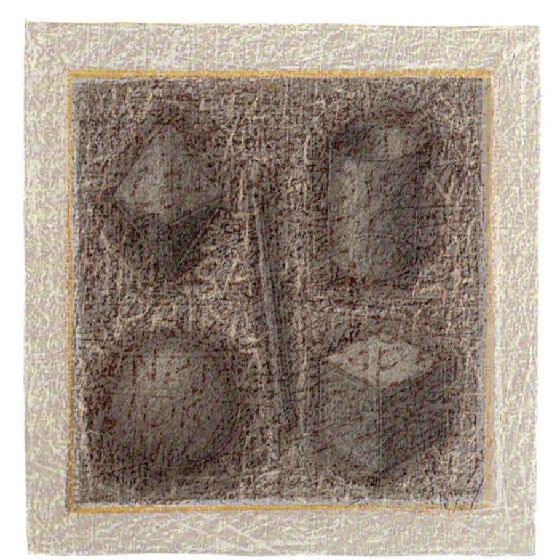 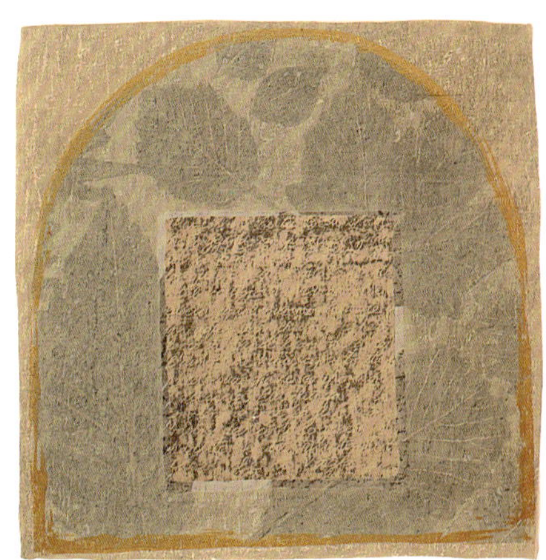

Excerpts from Hell
1997, set of six screenprints, each 12″ x 12″

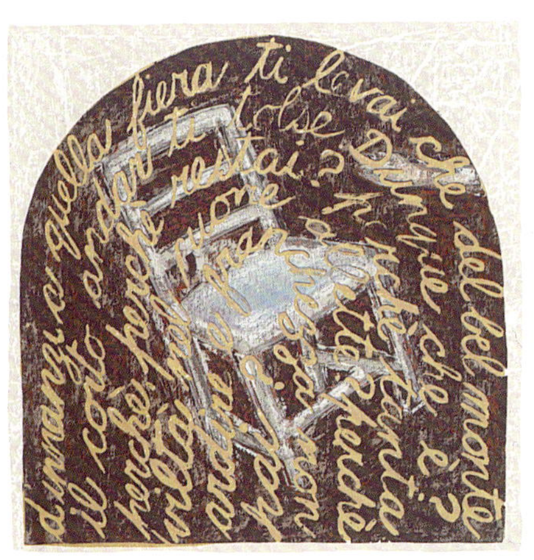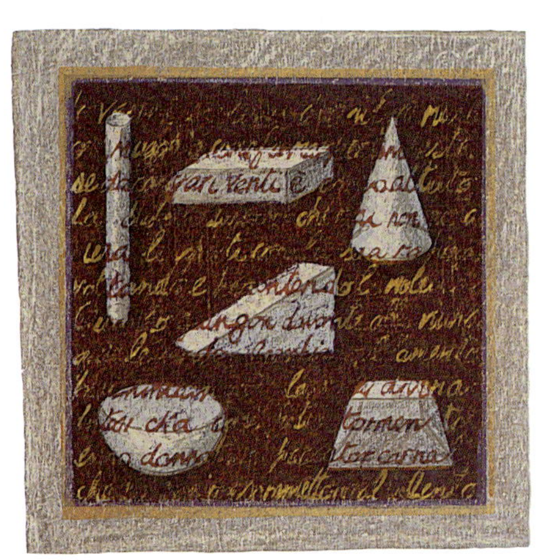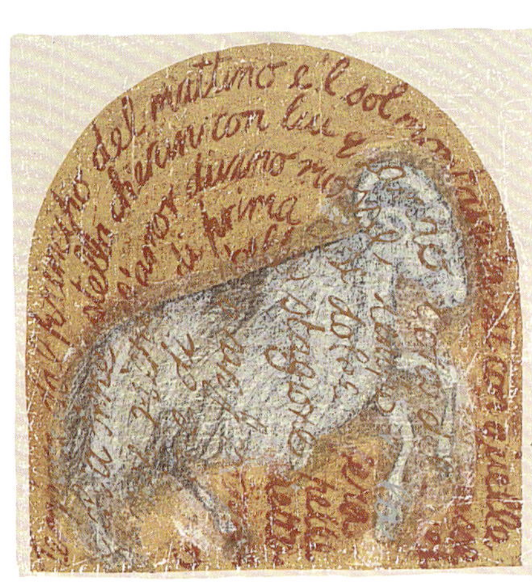

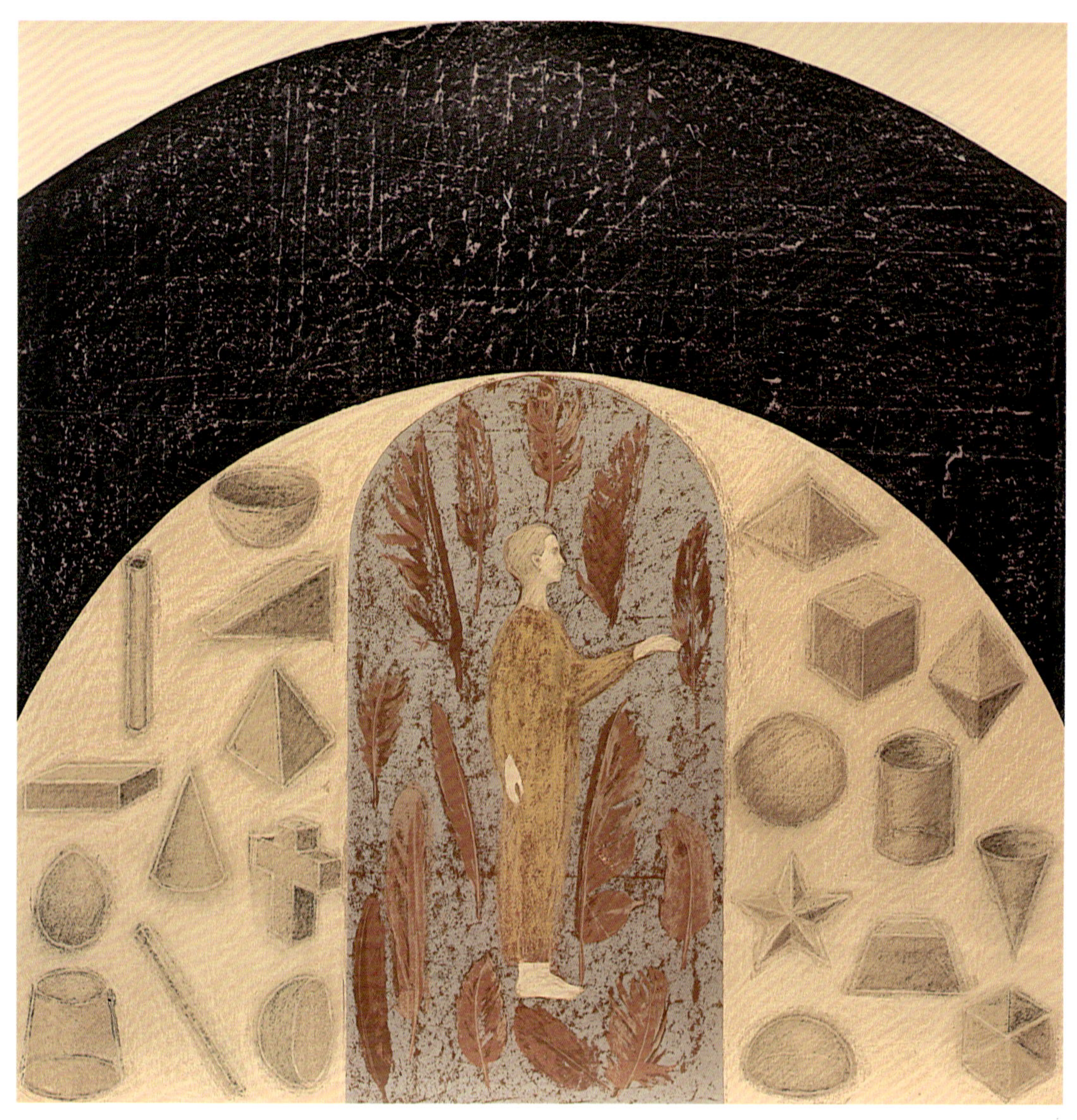

Of Passion I Reasoned a Vision   1997, screenprint, 30" x 30"

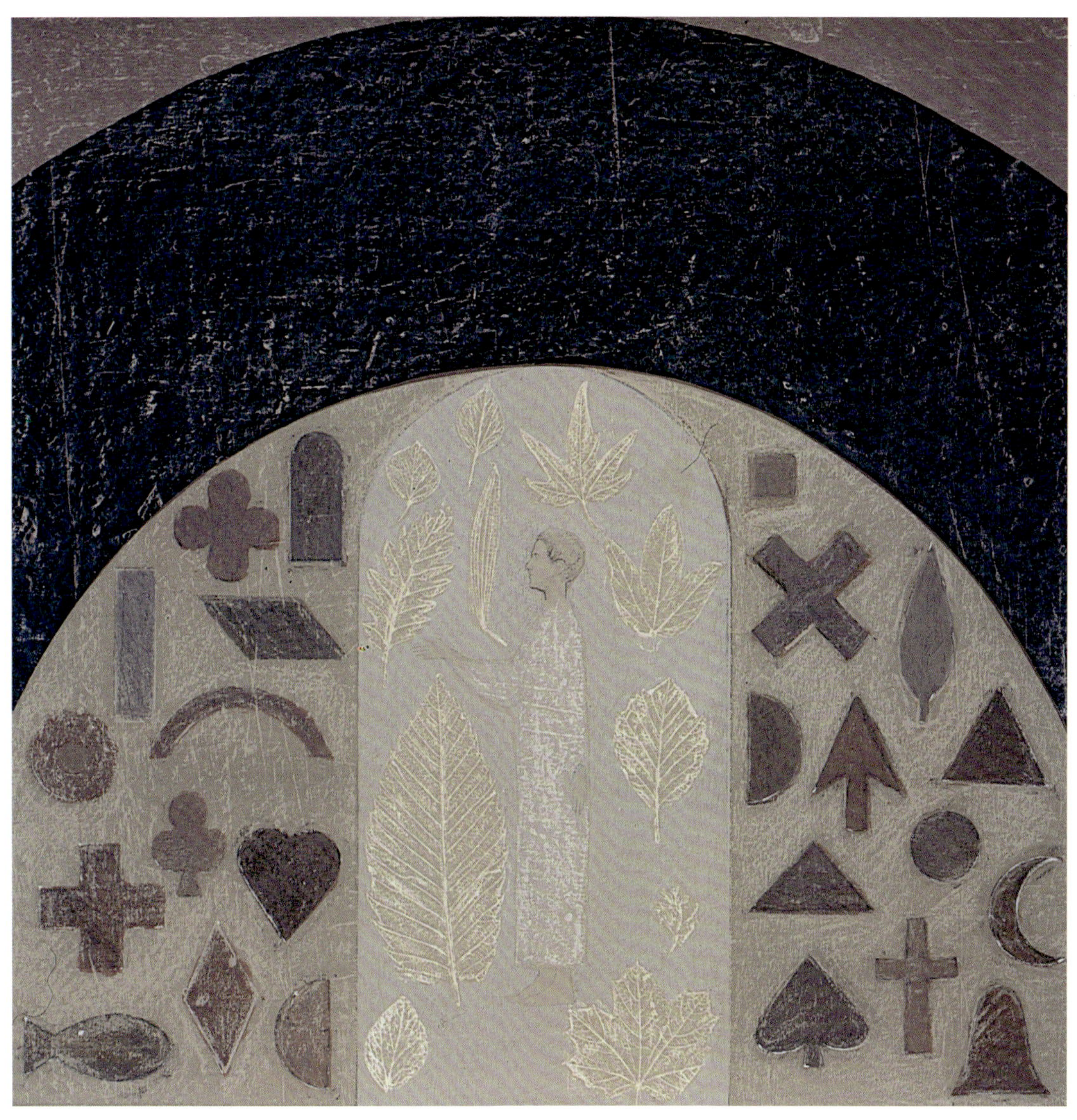

I was still (momentarily) in my argument with a life without contradiction   1997, screenprint, 30" x 30"

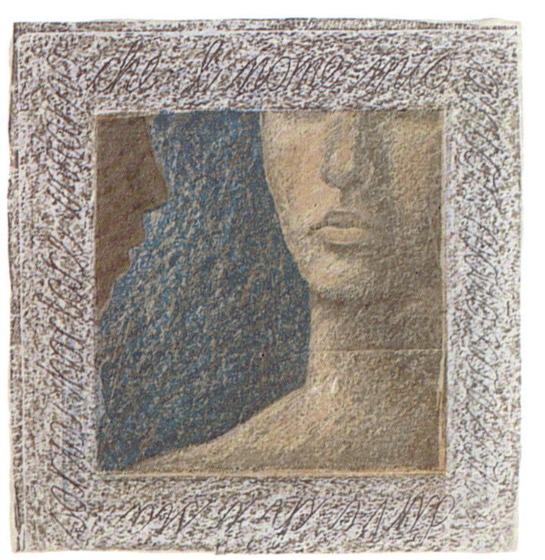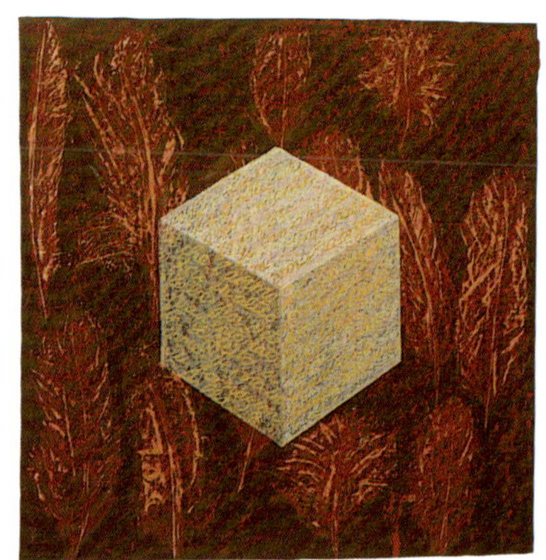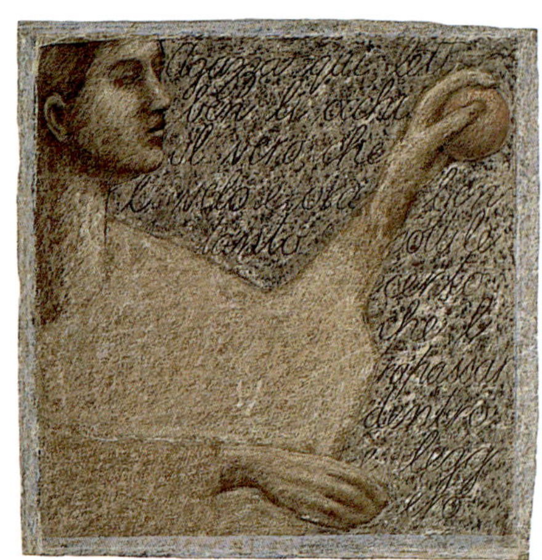

Excerpts from Purgatory
1997, set of six screenprints, each 12" x 12"

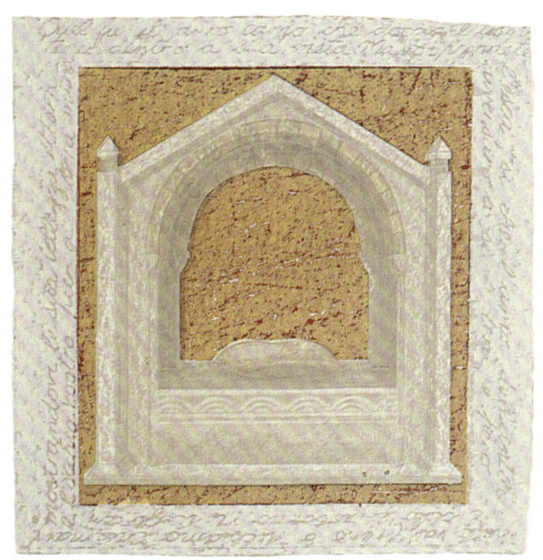 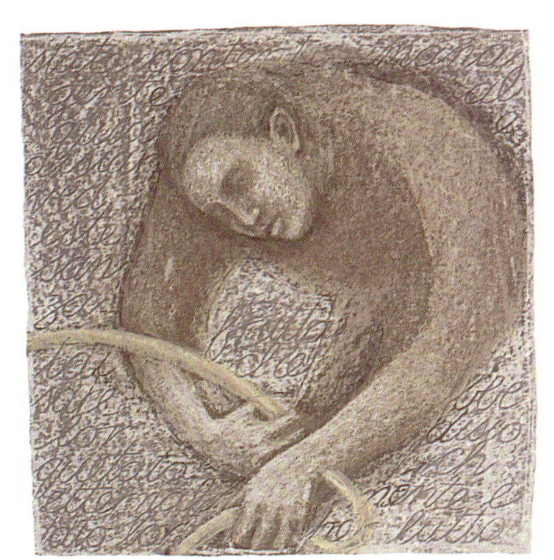 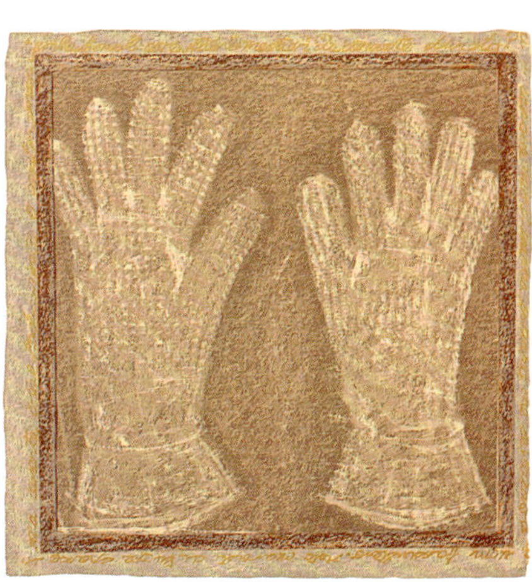

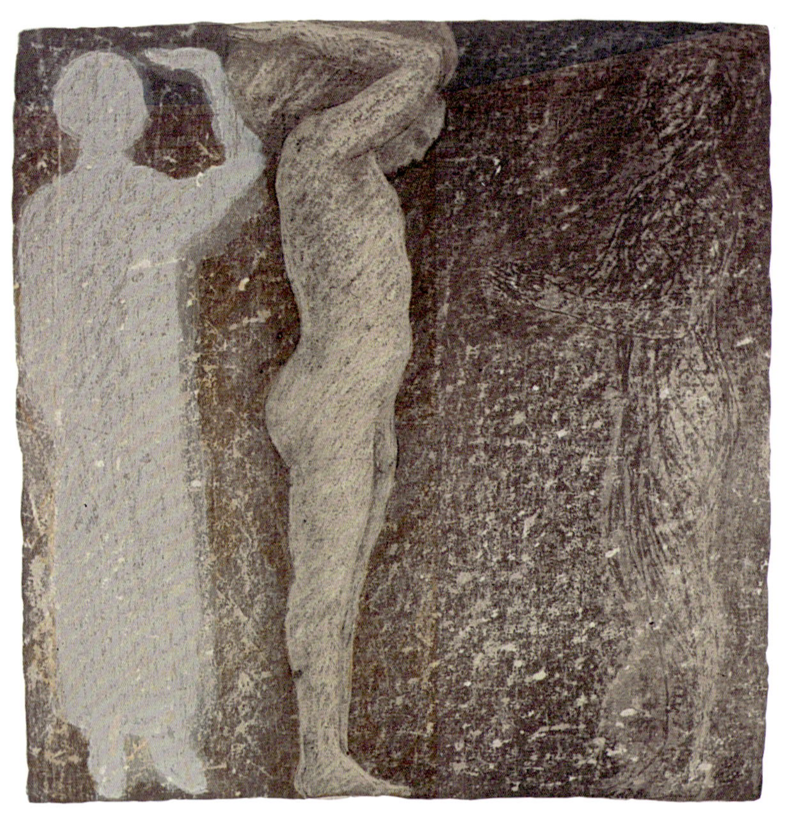

Erred Release
1997, screenprint, 14" x 14"

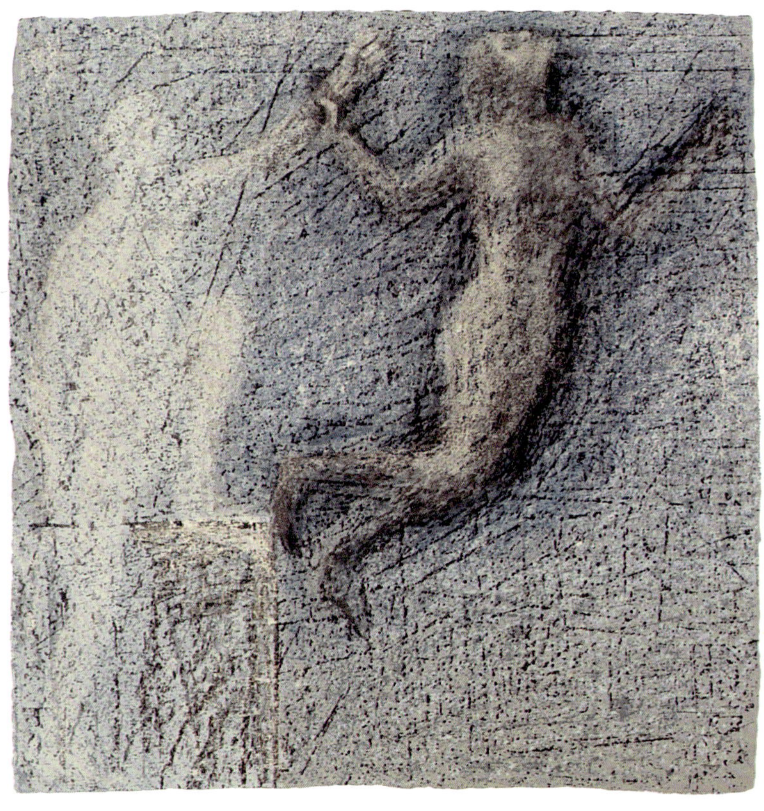

The Gravity of Wanting
1997, screenprint, 14" x 14"

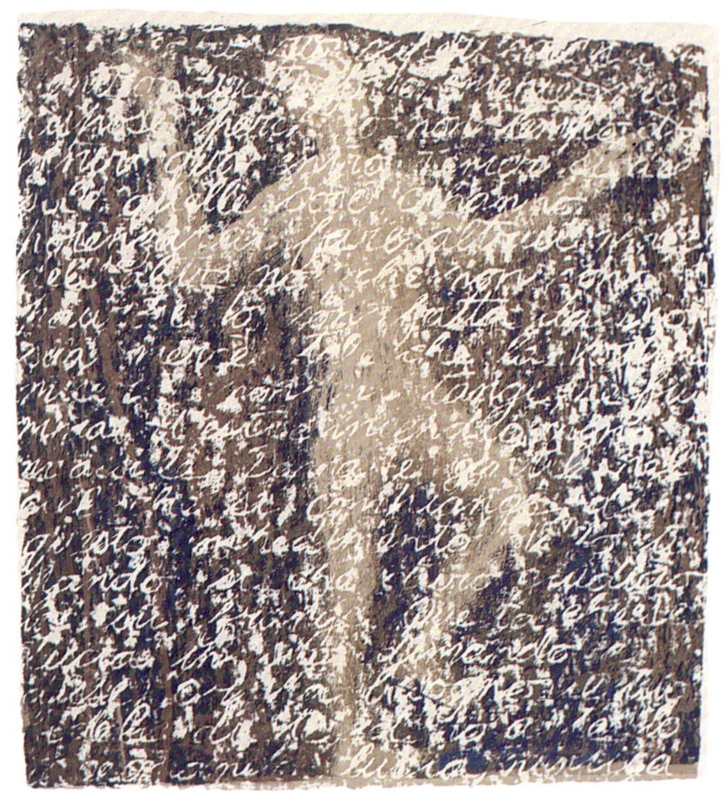

Figure I
1997, screenprint, 8" x 8"

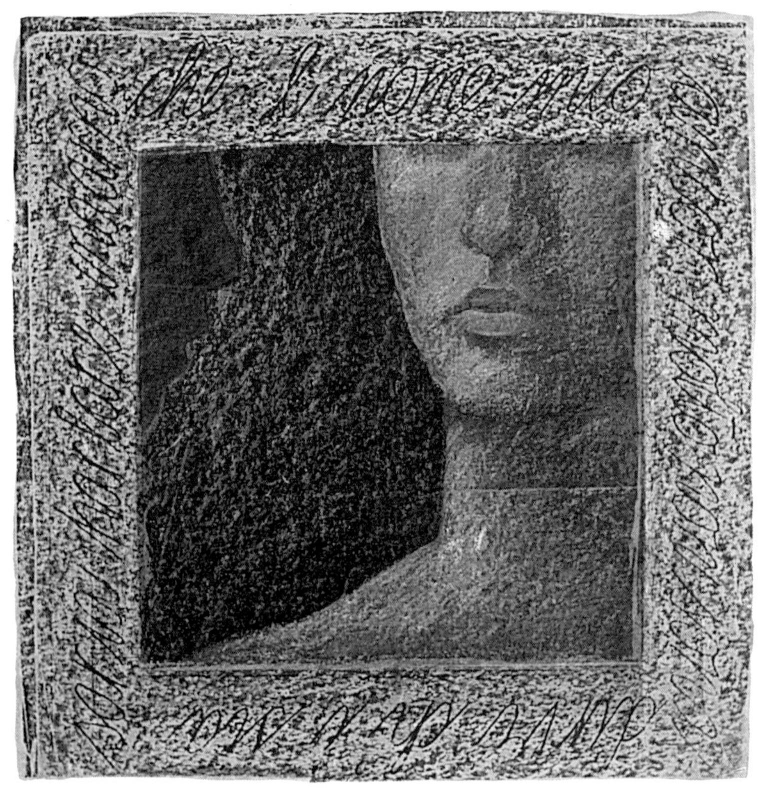

Excerpts from Purgatory
1997, one of six screenprints, each 12" x 12"

LIST OF ILLUSTRATIONS

all are screen prints
image size given in inches

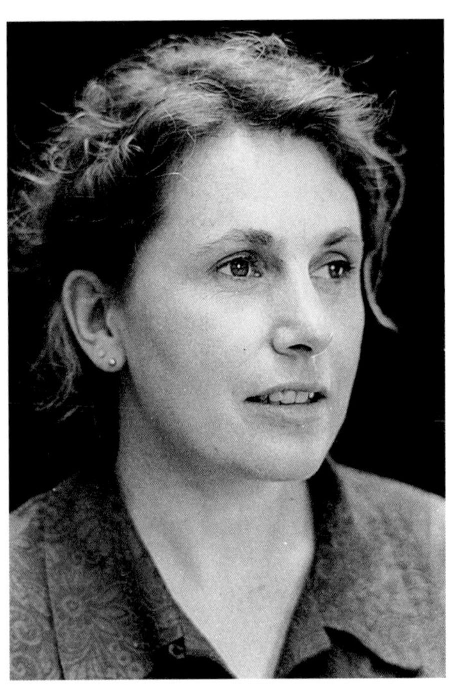

SIOBAN PIERCY

1957	Born in Oakham, England
1962	Moved to Ireland
1974-75	Ravensbourne College of Art & Design, Kent
1975-80	Crawford College of Art, Cork
1990-92	Royal College of Art, London (MA)
	Lectures in art full-time at Galway Regional Technical College
	Lives in Athenry, Co Galway

Solo Exhibitions

1997	Original Print Gallery, Dublin
1995	*Sióbán Piercy – Archaeologies*, Churchill College, Cambridge University
1993	Geoghegan Gallery, Galway
1987	Spanish Arch Gallery, Galway
1986	Triskel Arts Centre, Cork
1985	Belltable Arts Centre, Limerick
1978	Kilkenny Arts Week

Two-Person Exhibitions

1995	Columbus College, Georgia, USA
1994	Graphic Studio Gallery, Dublin
	Kilkenny Arts Week
1991	Merz Contemporary Art, London
1990	Riverrun Gallery, Limerick
1989	Winnower Gallery, Galway Arts Festival
	Dolan Moore Gallery, Athlone

Selected Group Exhibitions

1997   Cracow International Print Triennial
         Boyle Arts Festival
1996   Temple Bar International Print Exhibition, Dublin
         The Water is Wide, Galerie du Faouedic, Lorient
         (part of *l'Imaginaire Irlandais* festival)
         Contemporary Screen Printers, Original Print Gallery,
         Dublin
         Hardware Gallery, London
1995   Print Makers Council of Britain Open, London
1994   *Dispatches*, Crawford Municipal Art Gallery, Cork;
         Municipal Gallery, Perugia, Italy
         Works on Paper, Art Fair, New York
         Print Show, Blue Coat Chambers, Liverpool
93/95/96 *Print*, Rubicon Gallery, Dublin
1993   *Full Circle*, British School at Rome
         Intentional Print Biennial, Ljubljana, Slovina
1992   Open print exhibition, Bankside Gallery, London
         Flight, Crescent Arts Centre, Scarborough
         RCA Box Prints, Flowers East Gallery, London
         RCA Print Show, Marlborough Graphics, London
1991-92 *Four Galway Printmakers*, touring Galway, Athlone,
         Longford, Dublin, London
1991   RCA Print Show, Henry Moore Gallery, London
         Open print exhibition, Bankside Gallery, London
1990   Kochi International Exhibition of Prints, Japan
1989   Cleveland Drawing Biennial, UK
         International Mini-Print Exhibition, Barcelona
1980-81 Living Art, Dublin
1978-82 EV⁺A open exhibition, Limerick
1978   Graduate Show, Project Arts Centre, Dublin

Awards

1995   Printmakers Council of Britain Annual Open, London
         Dept of Foreign Affairs (exhibition at Cambridge)
1992/94 Arts Council / Aer Lingus Artflight
1993   British School at Rome (printmaking scholarship)
         SIPTU print commission

1992   Royal College of Art MA Degree Show (four awards)
1990   *Íontas* open exhibition, Sligo (print award)
1989   International Mini-Print Exhibition, Dublin
         National Portrait Exhibition, Arnotts, Dublin
         International Mini-Print Exhibition, Barcelona
1986   National Portrait Exhibition, Arnotts, Dublin
1978   EV⁺A open exhibition, Limerick (painting award)
1976   The Cork Art Society Student Award

Public Collections

The Arts Council / An Chomhairle Ealaíon; AIB Bank; Boyle Civic
Collection; Churchill College, Cambridge University; Columbus
College, Georgia, USA; Galway Regional Technical College;
Kilkenny County Library; Kerry County Library; Limerick Arts
Society Collection; Office of Public Works; RTÉ, Cork; SIPTU;
Tralee Regional Technical College; Tussauds Collection, London;
University College Cork

PROFILES

Profiles is a series of medium-format books on Irish artists from Gandon Editions, edited by John O'Regan.

Each volume in the series carries two major texts – an essay and an interview with the artist – and is heavily illustrated in colour. They are of a standard design and pagination, with 48 pages in a 22.5 cm square format, and retail at £7.50 paperback.

already published

Profile 1 – PAULINE FLYNN
essays by Paul M O'Reilly and Gus Gibney
ISBN 0946641 722
Gandon Editions, 1996   19 col + 3 b/w illus

Profile 2 – SEÁN McSWEENEY
essay by Brian Fallon
interview by Aidan Dunne
ISBN 0946641 617
Gandon Editions, 1996   17 col + 6 b/w illus

Profile 3 – EILÍS O'CONNELL
essay by Caoimhín Mac Giolla Léith
interview by Medb Ruane
ISBN 0946641 870
Gandon Editions, 1997   27 col + 8 b/w illus

Profile 4 – SIOBÁN PIERCY
essay by Aidan Dunne
interview by Vera Ryan
ISBN 0946641 900
Gandon Editions, 1997   32 col + 6 b/w illus

titles in preparation

Profile 5 – MARY LOHAN
essay by Noel Sheridan
interview by Aidan Dunne
ISBN 0946641 889
Gandon Editions, Oct 1997

Profile 6 – ALICE MAHER
essay by Medb Ruane
interview by Medb Ruane
ISBN 0946641 935
Gandon Editions, Nov 1997

to be continued …